The
KNOWLEDGE OF
LIFE

W I T N E S S   L E E

Living Stream Ministry
Anaheim, CA • www.lsm.org

First Edition, 1973.

ISBN 978-0-87083-419-6

Published by

Living Stream Ministry
2431 W. La Palma Ave., Anaheim, CA 92801 U.S.A.
P. O. Box 2121, Anaheim, CA 92814 U.S.A.

Printed in the United States of America

13 14 15 16 17 / 13 12 11 10 9 8

CONTENTS

All Scripture quotations, unless otherwise noted,
are from the American Standard Version (1901).

INTRODUCTION

Although we know that God's desire and intention is to gain a corporate man, having His image, manifesting His glory, and possessing His authority to deal with His enemy that He Himself may gain eternal rest, yet very few know that this great desire and intention of God can only be attained through His own life. Even fewer have touched this matter of knowing and experiencing this life which accomplishes the purpose of God. Therefore, the saints today are rather weak and immature. Although there are many seeking ones, yet very few have found the way of life. Many people have even mistaken zeal, knowledge, power, and gifts, etc., for life.

We thank God that in these last days of urgent need God has made manifest through our brother's messages the line of His wonderful and hidden life, and thus made it possible for every believer to see and touch this matter. These messages may be considered a crystallization of the cream of the saints' knowledge and experience of life in the past two thousand years, plus our brother's thirty years of personal experience; they are indeed complete and superb. The contents of these messages are divided into two main parts. The first part discusses the knowledge of life and is divided into fourteen main points which show the characteristics of life and its various principles of working. The second part* discusses the experiences of life and is divided into nineteen items which explain the experiences in the various stages of the spiritual life and the way of pursuing life. If we pursue and practice these lessons one by one, we will be enabled to rise in a straight line and rapidly attain to the stage of the maturity of life.

Therefore, these messages have made practical the almost

---

* The second part has already been published by the Living Stream Ministry entitled *The Experience of Life.*

invisible and untouchable science of life. All those saints who love the Lord and pursue after the growth of life need to read these messages.

Dr. Y. L. Chang

November 1956
Taipei, Taiwan, Republic of China

FOURTEEN POINTS CONCERNING LIFE

We shall use fourteen chapters which cover fourteen main points to see from every side what life is and some matters relating to life. In this book we build a foundation on the knowledge of life. We have covered the matter concerning the experience of life in another volume.*

* The Experience of Life, published by the Living Stream Ministry.

CHAPTER ONE

WHAT IS LIFE?

First we shall see what life is. In order to know life, we must know what life is. It is rather difficult to explain; hence, we really need the mercy of the Lord. According to the teaching of the Bible, at least six points should be mentioned in order to make this subject clear.

I. ONLY THE LIFE OF GOD IS LIFE

When explaining what life is, we must first be clear about one thing—the kind of life in the whole universe which can be counted as life. First John 5:12 says: "He that hath the Son hath the life; he that hath not the Son of God hath not the life." John 3:36 also says: "He that believeth on the Son hath eternal life; but he that obeyeth not the Son shall not see life." These two scriptures tell us that unless man has the life of God, he does not have life. This shows us that in the eyes of God, only His life is life; besides that, no other life can be counted as life. Thus, when the life of God is mentioned in the Bible, it is treated as if it is the unique life (John 1:4; 10:10; 11:25; 14:6; etc.).

Only the life of God is life, and other lives are not counted as life, because only the life of God is divine and eternal.

What does *divine* mean? Being divine means being of God, having the nature of God, or being transcendent and distinctive from all others. Only God is God, only God has the nature of God, and only God is transcendent and distinctive; therefore, only God is divine. The life of God is God Himself (later we shall consider this point), and since it is God Himself, it naturally has the nature of God. For example, a gold cup is gold, and since it is gold, it has the nature of gold; in fact, gold is its nature. Similarly the life of God is God Himself and has

God's nature; God is the nature of His life. Since the life of
God is God and has the nature of God, the life of God is
divine.

What does *eternal* mean? Eternal means uncreated, without
beginning or ending, existing by itself and ever, unchangeably
existing. Only God is uncreated; only He is "from eternity to
eternity" (Psa. 90:2, original text), that is, without beginning
or ending. He is "I am that I am" (Exo. 3:14), and always "the
same" (Psa. 102:27). Since God Himself is such, so also is the
life which is God Himself. The life of God, just as God Himself,
is uncreated, without beginning or ending, self-existing and
ever-existing, and never changing; therefore, the life of God is
eternal. Hence the Scriptures speak of God's life as eternal
life.

Since being both divine and eternal are the nature of
God and show forth the characteristics of God Himself, they
are also the nature of His life and portray the characteristics
of His life. However, not only is being divine a characteristic of God's life, but it is even more the essence of His life,
whereas being eternal is only a characteristic of the life of
God. Let us look again at the illustration of the gold cup.
Its nature is both gold and rust-resistant. However, gold
not only characterizes the cup but is also its very essence,
whereas its nature of being rust-resistant is due to its being
gold. Likewise, the reason God's life is eternal is that it is
divine. (Being divine signifies not only that which is of God,
but God Himself.) God's life is eternal because it is divine. In
the universe, no created life has the divine nature; therefore,
no created life is eternal. Only the nature of God's uncreated
life is divine and eternal. Since the nature of God's life is
such, naturally God's life itself is also such. God's life is eternal because it is divine. In the whole universe, only God's life
is both divine and eternal; therefore, only God's life is considered life.

Only the life that is both divine and eternal can be
counted as life because life denotes something which is living,
and all that is considered life must be something that is
immortal. That which is immortal is unchangeable; it
remains the same and continues living even after passing

through any kind of blow or destruction. A life which is subject to death and change and is unable to suffer any blow or destruction is neither eternal, immortal, nor unchangeable, and therefore cannot be considered life. That which is life must be something that lives forever and never changes. Only that which is eternal can be such. Then, what is it that is eternal? Only that which is divine! That which is divine is of God, and this is God Himself. God Himself is without beginning or ending, self-existing and ever-existing; therefore, He is eternal. Because only that which is divine is eternal and only that which is eternal can live eternally without change, only that which is both divine and eternal can be counted as life.

All kinds of life in the universe, whether of angel, man, animal or plant, are mortal and changeable; hence, they are not eternal. They do not have the nature of God, nor are they divine. Only the life of God has the nature of God; therefore, it is divine and eternal, immortal and unchangeable, impossible to be held by death, and indestructible (Acts 2:24; Heb. 7:16). No matter what kind of blow or destruction it undergoes, it remains unchanged and stays forever the same. In the universe, beside the life of God, no other life can be such. Therefore, from the standpoint of eternity, only the life of God is life. It not only has the name of life, but also the reality of life, and thus it completely fulfills the meaning of life. Other lives are only life in name, not in reality; thus, they are unable to meet the criteria of immortality and unchangeability of life, and cannot be considered as life. Hence, according to the divine and eternal nature of the life of God, God's life is the unique life in the whole universe.*

II. LIFE IS THE FLOWING OUT OF GOD

Concerning what life is, we must first see that only the life

---

* Because the life of God is the unique life, whenever the New Testament in the original Greek speaks of this life, it always uses the word *zoe*, which refers to the highest life (John 1:4; 1 John 1:2; 5:12; etc.). Beside this, the original text of the New Testament also uses (1) *bios* to speak of the life of the flesh (Luke 8:43; 21:4; etc.), and (2) *psuche* to speak of the soul life or the natural life of man (Matt. 16:25-26; Luke 9:24; etc.).

of God is life. Then we must see that life is the flowing out of God. Revelation 22:1-2 speaks of a river of water of life flowing out of the throne of God, and in the river of water of life is the tree of life. Both the water of life and the tree of life signify life. Therefore, we are shown clearly here that life is that which flows out from God. Hence, we can say that life is the flowing out of God.

We have already seen that life must be divine and eternal. Since God is God, naturally He is divine. And the Bible also says that God is eternal. Hence, since God is both divine and eternal, He is life. Therefore, God flowing out is life.

According to the divine and eternal nature of God Himself, God is life. But if God does not flow out, although in respect to Himself He is life, yet to us He is not life. He must flow out; then He will be life to us. His flowing out passes through two steps. The first step is His becoming flesh. This enables Him to flow out from heaven into the midst of men and manifest Himself as life (John 1:1, 14, 4). Therefore, the Bible speaks of this on the one hand as His being "manifested in the flesh" (1 Tim. 3:16), and on the other hand as the "life which was manifested" (1 John 1:2). Hence, when He was in the flesh, He said that He is life (John 14:6). Although in the first step of His flowing out He could manifest Himself as life to us, He could not be received by us as life; therefore, He must take the second step of flowing out. His second step of flowing out is His being nailed on the cross. Through death, the body of flesh which He took was broken, thus enabling Him to flow out from the flesh and become the living water of life to be received by us (John 19:34; 4:10, 14). The rock in the Old Testament typified Him; it was smitten, and from it came living water to be obtained by the people of Israel (Exo. 17:6; 1 Cor. 10:4). He became flesh in order that He may be a grain of wheat which contains life. He was crucified so that He could flow out from the husk of flesh into us—His many fruits— and become our life (John 12:24).

Thus, the life we receive from God is the flowing out of God Himself. This life flowing into us, from our side, is the flowing in of God, and from God's side, it is the flowing out of God. Then, when this life flows out of us, it is again the flowing out of God. This flowing out of God began from His throne: first it flowed into Jesus the Nazarene; then it passed through the cross and flowed into the apostles; then it flowed out of the apostles as rivers of living water (John 7:38); it has flowed through the saints of all ages, and eventually it has flowed into us. Out from us it will flow to millions more and on to eternity, flowing forever without ceasing, just as is spoken in Revelation 22:1-2 and John 4:14.

The waters mentioned in Ezekiel 47 symbolize this flowing out of God. Whithersoever the waters flow, all things shall have life. Likewise, wherever this flowing out of God comes, there shall be life, for this flowing out is life itself. When this flowing out flows to eternity, then eternity will be filled with the condition of life and become an eternity of life.

At the very beginning, when the Bible speaks of life, it shows us a flowing river (Gen. 2:9-14). At the end in Revelation, we are shown that, as far as we are concerned, all things relating to life, whether the water of life or the tree of life, flow out from God. This speaks clearly that, to us, life is the flowing out of God Himself. God flowed out from heaven, and through the flesh He flowed into our midst as the life which was manifested to us. Then He flowed out from the flesh into us as the life which we have received.

III. LIFE IS THE CONTENT OF GOD

Concerning what life is, the third point we should know is that life is the content of God. Since life is the flowing out of God, it therefore is the content of God, for the flowing out of God is from God Himself, and God Himself is the content of God.

Since the content of God is God Himself, this content is all that God is, or the fullness of the Godhead. The Bible tells us that all the fullness of the Godhead is in Christ (Col. 2:9). This is because Christ as God's embodiment was manifested to be the life of man. This life contains all the fullness of the Godhead, which is all that God is. All that God is, is in this life. God's being God hinges on this life. Therefore, this life is the content of God, the fullness of the Godhead. When we receive this life, we receive the content of God, and we receive all that is in God. This life within us is what God is. Today it is in this life that God becomes our all and is our all; it is in this life that God becomes our God and is our God. Since this life in Christ is the fullness of the Godhead and the content of God Himself, so also in us it is the fullness of the Godhead and the content of God Himself.

IV. LIFE IS GOD HIMSELF

We have seen that life is the flowing out of God, and life is the content of God. The flowing out of God issues from God Himself, and the content of God is also God Himself. Since life is both the flowing out of God and the content of God, naturally life is God Himself. This is the fourth point we should know concerning what life is.

In John 14:6 the Lord Jesus says that He is life. After He said this, from verse 7 to 11, He made known to the disciples that He and God are one—and when He speaks this word, it is God speaking in Him. He is God become flesh; and He is God in the flesh (John 1:1, 14; 1 Tim. 3:16). When He says He is life, it is God who says God is life. Hence His words show us that life is the very God Himself.

We should pay attention to the fact that the Bible seldom uses the term "the life of God." The teaching of the Bible mainly reveals to us that God *is* life; it speaks mostly of God *as* life; seldom does it mention "the life *of* God." It tells us God *is* our life and speaks of God *as* our life; it almost never says that God wants us to receive "His life." The life *of* God is different from God *is* life or God *as* life. *The life of God* does not necessarily imply the whole of God Himself, whereas *God is life* or *God as life* denotes the complete God Himself. Strictly speaking, when we receive life, we receive not the life *of* God, but God *as* life. Not only did God give us His life; He Himself came to be our life. Because God Himself is life, His life is His very self.

Then what is life? Life is God Himself. What does it mean to have life? To have life is to have God Himself. What does it mean to live out life? To live out life is to live out God Himself. Life is not different in the least from God. If it were, then it would not be life. We should understand this clearly. It is not sufficient merely to know that we have life; we must know further that this life we have is God Himself. It is not sufficient only to know that we should live out life; we must also know that the life we should live out is God Himself.

Brothers and sisters, actually what is the life that we should live out? What do we live out when we live out life? Is the living out of love, humility, gentleness, and patience the living out of life? No! Because neither love, humility, gentleness, nor patience is life; neither is any goodness or virtue life. Only God Himself is life. Thus, to live out such virtues is not to live out life. Only the living out of God Himself is the living out of life. If the love, humility, gentleness, and patience which we live out are not the flowing out of God or the manifestation of God, they are not life. Any goodness or virtue that we live out, unless it is the expression of God through us, is not life. The good virtues we live out must be the flowing out of God, the manifestation of God, and the expression of God; then we are living out life; for life is God Himself.

Colossians 2:9 and Ephesians 3:19 show us the fullness of God. The life which we receive is this full God. Therefore, this life is also full. In it there is love and light, humility and gentleness, patience and forbearance, sympathy and understanding. All the goodness and virtues that are in God are in this life. Therefore, this life can live out all these virtues from us. To live out these virtues is to live out God, because this life is God. Although this life, when it is lived out, has many manifestations, such as love, humility, gentleness, and patience, yet these are all expressions of God, for they are all lived out from God. That which is lived out from God is the expression of God, or the expression of life, because God is life and life is God.

V. LIFE IS CHRIST

The Bible shows us that life is God Himself. It shows us even more that life is Christ. Life was God; then God became flesh, which is Christ. Therefore, Christ is God, and Christ also is life (1 John 5:12). The life which was God, the life that God is, is in Him (John 1:4). Hence, Christ said again and again that He is life (John 14:6; 11:25), and that He came to earth that man may have life (John 10:10). Therefore, the Bible says that he that has Him has life (1 John 5:12), and that He in us is our life (Col. 3:4).

Just as life is God Himself, so also life is Christ. Just as having life is having God Himself, so also having life is having Christ. Just as to live out life is to live out God Himself, so also to live out life is to live out Christ. Just as life is not different in the least from God, likewise life is not different in the least from Christ. Just as a slight deviation from God is not life, likewise a slight deviation from Christ is not life. For Christ is God being life. It is through Christ and as Christ that God is manifested as life. Hence, Christ is life and life is Christ.

VI. LIFE IS THE HOLY SPIRIT

After the Lord Jesus said He was life in John 14:6, He made known to His disciples not only that He and God are one (vv. 7-11), but also that the Holy Spirit and He are also one (vv. 16-20).* From verses 7 to 11 He showed us that He is the embodiment of God—He is in God, and God is in Him. Hence, His being life means that God is life. From verses 16 to 20, He further revealed that the Holy Spirit is His embodiment, His other form; and when His physical presence leaves us, this Spirit of reality Who is Himself as another comforter comes into us and abides with us. This Spirit living in us and abiding with us is just He Himself living in us as our life that we may live. These two passages therefore show us that it is by God being in Him and Him being the Holy Spirit that He is life. God is in Him as life, and He is the Holy Spirit as life. Him being life is God being life, and is also the Holy Spirit being life. Thus, John 4:10, 14 tells us that the living water which He gives is the eternal life. John 7:38-39 further tells us that the living water which flows out from us is the Holy

---

* In verses 16 and 17 the Lord referred to the Holy Spirit as "he," but in verse 18, He changed the pronoun from "he" to "I." By changing the "he" to "I" the Lord was saying that "he" is "I." This reveals that the Holy Spirit He spoke of in verses 16 and 17 is He Himself.

Spirit which we received. This discloses that the Holy Spirit is the eternal life. The Holy Spirit we receive is the eternal life we experience, or Christ being experienced by us as life. The eternal life, or Christ as life, is to be experienced by us as the Holy Spirit. For this reason, the Holy Spirit is called "the Spirit of life" (Rom. 8:2).

The Holy Spirit is "the Spirit of life" because God and Christ being life hinges on Him. He and life are united as one and cannot be separated. He is of life, and life is of Him. Life is His content, and He is the reality of life. Speaking more accurately, He is not only the reality of life, but also life itself.

We all know that God is a triune God—Father, Son, and Spirit. The Father is in the Son; the Son is the Spirit. The Father in the Son is manifested among men; therefore, the Son is the manifestation of the Father. The Son as the Spirit enters into man; therefore, the Spirit is the entering in of the Son. The Father is the source of life, the very life itself. Since the Son is the manifestation of the Father (1 Tim. 3:16), He is the manifestation of life (1 John 1:2). And since the Spirit is the entering in of the Son, He is the entering in of life. Life originally is the Father; in the Son, it is manifested among man; and as the Spirit, it enters into man for man to experience. Thus, the Spirit becomes the Spirit of life. Since the Spirit is the Spirit of life, man can receive life through the Spirit, and when man sets his mind on the Spirit, it is life (Rom. 8:6). Since the Spirit is the Spirit of life, when man exercises his spirit to touch the Spirit, he touches life. When he contacts the Spirit, he contacts life, and when he obeys the Spirit, he experiences life.

Thus, in summary, life is the Triune God. But to us, life is not the Triune God in heaven, but the Triune God flowing out. This flowing out of the Triune God means that His content, which is Himself, first flowed out through Christ; then it flowed out as the Spirit to be received by us as life. Thus, when we touch God in Christ as the Spirit, we touch life, for life is God in Christ as the Spirit.

CHAPTER TWO

WHAT IS THE EXPERIENCE OF LIFE?

We will now ask the second question: What is the experience of life? Once we have seen what life is, we may easily know what the experience of life is.

I. EXPERIENCING GOD

We have seen that life is God Himself. God Himself flowing into us, being received and experienced by us, is life. Therefore, to experience God is to experience life. All experience of life is the experiencing and touching of God. Any experience that does not touch God is not an experience of life.

For example, some repentance is not due to God's enlightenment, but to man's own introspection. Since it does not cause man to touch God, it is not an experience of life. Repentance which results from God's enlightenment surely will cause man to touch God, and is therefore an experience of life.

That which is derived from man's own behavior is not an experience of life. It is artificial and of man's own work; it is not the result of God passing through man nor man passing through God; therefore, it cannot be counted as an experience of life.

What then can be considered an experience of life? An experience which results from God passing through man and man passing through Him is considered an experience of life. For example: in our prayer we meet God, become enlightened, see our own fault, and deal with it before God. It is not that we detect our own fault, but rather, when we draw near to God, we are inwardly met by God, and thereby we see our own fault. God is light; hence when we meet Him, we see our fault in His light. We naturally confess to God and ask for the cleansing of the Lord's blood. As a consequence, God passes through us, and we also pass through God. Such experience causes us to experience God; therefore, it is the experience of life.

All experiences of life are from God and are His working within us; therefore, they can cause us to touch God and experience Him. All experience that is not such is not the experience of life, for life is God, and to experience life is to experience God. Hence, any such experience of God will show forth life (Phil. 2:13-16).

II. EXPERIENCING CHRIST

To experience life undoubtedly is to experience God, yet God is in Christ to be experienced by us. Christ is God's manifestation and embodiment; He is God becoming our experience. Therefore, all our experience of God is the experience of Christ and is in Christ. Thus, since to experience life is to experience God, it is also to experience Christ.

Though God is life, He cannot be our life except He be in Christ and become Christ, and thus be experienced by us. In order to be experienced by us, He must be our life. But He cannot be our life while in heaven, in the light which no man can approach (1 Tim. 6:16). Furthermore, in order to be our life, He must have our human nature. His divine life must be mingled with human nature so that it can be united with us, who possess the human nature, and be our life. Therefore, He came out from heaven, became flesh, and mingled with human nature. Thus, God became Christ and becomes our life in the human nature for us to experience Him. When we experience Him as our life, we experience Christ.

In short, when we experience Christ, we will experience the following aspects:

A. Christ Revealed in Us (Gal. 1:16)

This is our initial experience of Christ when we are saved. We experience God revealing Christ in us through the Holy Spirit, thus enabling us to know and receive Him as our life and our all.

B. Christ Living in Us (Gal. 2:20)

This is our continuous experience of Christ living in us as our life after we are saved. In other words, we experience Christ abiding in us and living for us. This, the continuous experience of Christ in our daily life as saints, constitutes the major part of our experience of Christ.

C. Christ Being Formed in Us (Gal. 4:19)

This is our letting all that is of Christ be the element of our inward life, that Christ may grow and be formed in us. Christ is in us not only that we may experience Him as our life, as the One who is living for us, but that we may experience Him even more as our all, thus enabling Him to grow and be formed in our life that His life may reach maturity in us.

D. Christ Being Magnified in Our Body (Phil. 1:20-21)

This is our letting all that is of Christ become the expression of our outward living, that Christ may be manifested outwardly. Whether it be by life or by death, in any circumstance we let Christ be magnified in our body. In other words, for us to live is Christ. This, of course, is a somewhat deeper experience of Christ: it is not only experiencing Him being formed within us, but also experiencing Him being magnified out from us. Christ being formed in us is the maturity of the inward life; it is then that we have all that is His as our inner elements. Christ being magnified in our body is the expression of the outward living; by this we allow all that is His to be our outward manifestation. Hence, in this experience, we experience Christ not only as the elements of our inward life, but also as the manifestation of our outward living.

E. Full of the Measure of the Stature of the Fullness of Christ (Eph. 4:13)

This means that we all, that is, the Body, experience Christ till we are full of the elements and constitution of Christ; thus, we grow and are full of the stature of the fullness of Christ. This, of course, is a corporate experience of Christ in full.

F. Transformed into the Image of Christ
(2 Cor. 3:18)

Our experience of Christ can transform us until we are like Him. This begins with our experience of Christ being revealed in us and goes on until our body is redeemed (Rom. 8:23). The more we experience Him, the more we are changed, until even our body is changed in form to the likeness of His glorious body (Phil. 3:21). By that time, we will be completely conformed to His image (Rom. 8:29) and we shall be "like Him" (1 John 3:2). We shall then experience Him in a full way.

All that pertains to the life within us and the sanctified living out from us should be our experience of Christ. Because Christ is our life, He is also our sanctification (Col. 3:4; 1 Cor. 1:30). Any experience which pertains to our inward life ought to be Christ living within us; moreover, our outward sanctified living should be Christ living out through us. All our experience of life should be the experience of Christ. Not only should such great experiences of life as dying with Christ, being resurrected with Him, and ascending with Him be our experience, but even the small experiences of life in our daily living should all be the experience of Christ. Whether it be deliverance from sin or overcoming the world, the living out of sanctification and spirituality, or the living out of love and humility, all should be the experience of Christ. Even the little forbearance and patience we have toward others should be the experience of Christ.

To experience Christ is to let Christ live both within us and out from us. To experience Christ is to take Christ as life and thus to live by Christ. To experience Christ means that all our living and actions are Christ Himself living out and acting out from us. To experience Christ is to experience the power of His resurrection (Phil. 3:10)—this is the experience of Him as life; therefore, such an experience is also the experience of life.

III. EXPERIENCING THE HOLY SPIRIT

In John 14, after the Lord Jesus tells us that He is life (v. 6), He shows us not only that He and God are one, that He is in God, God is in Him, and His being life means that God is life (vv. 7-11); not only that the Holy Spirit and He are also one, that the Holy Spirit entering into us and abiding with us is Christ living in us to be our life (vv. 16-19); but also that He as the Holy Spirit entering into us and living in us means that both He and God as the Spirit enter into us and abide with us as our life (vv. 20-23). Simply speaking, after the Lord said that He is life, He shows us three things: (1) God is in Him as life, (2) He is the Holy Spirit as life, and (3) the Triune God enters into us as life. Thus, when we experience life, not only do we experience God, not only do we experience Christ, but we also experience the Holy Spirit. Actually, the Holy Spirit is both God and Christ as life being experienced by us, or God in Christ as life being experienced by us.

As Christ is the embodiment of God, so the Holy Spirit is the embodiment of Christ. God as life is in Christ, and Christ as life is the Holy Spirit. We experience God in Christ, and we experience Christ as the Holy Spirit. Thus, as the experience of life is the experience of God and Christ, so also is it the experience of the Holy Spirit.

God is life, Christ is God coming as life, and the Holy Spirit is the Spirit of God in Christ as life, or the Spirit of life (Rom. 8:2). It is this Spirit of life, the Holy Spirit, that causes us to experience all the content of God in Christ as life. It is this Holy Spirit of life who causes us to experience the indwelling of Christ, and it is this Holy Spirit of life who causes us to experience the resurrection power of God in Christ (Rom. 8:9-11). It is this Holy Spirit of life who leads us to put to death the evil deeds of the body, and it is this Holy Spirit of life who prays in us (Rom. 8:13, 26). All our experiences of life, whether deep or shallow, are produced by the Holy Spirit; therefore, they are all experiences of this Holy Spirit of life.

Romans 8:9-11 shows us not only that it is the Holy Spirit who enables us to experience the indwelling of Christ and the resurrection power of God, but also that it is the Holy Spirit abiding in us who causes us to experience that life is Christ, and it is God abiding in us who causes us to experience life. Thus, the life of God in Christ is experienced by us through the Holy Spirit. Hence, in order to experience this life, we must experience the Holy Spirit; and when we experience this life, we experience the Holy Spirit.

Therefore, the experience of life is the experience of the Triune God, or the experience of God in Christ and Christ as the Holy Spirit to be our life. The Holy Spirit working in us, leading us to experience Christ and to experience God in Christ—this is the experience of life. When, in the Holy Spirit, we pass through God and Christ and allow God and Christ to pass through us, this is the experience of life. Only such experience of the Holy Spirit, Christ, and God, is the experience of life. All that is otherwise cannot be counted as the experience of life. You can say that it is zeal, religious living, or self-improvement, but you cannot say that it is the experience of life. To experience life is to experience God, to experience Christ, and to experience the Holy Spirit. This is not something of our own doing or attempt at improvement; rather it is the issue of God moving in us, Christ living out through us, and the anointing of the Holy Spirit in us. May we pursue after this.

CHAPTER THREE

THE FIRST EXPERIENCE OF LIFE—
REGENERATION

We have seen what life is, and we have seen what the experience of life is. Now we come to see the first experience of life, which is regeneration. Regeneration is the first step of our experience of God's life; therefore, it is our first experience of God's life. This experience is very fundamental and extremely important. We shall use several points to look into it. First let us see:

I. WHY REGENERATION IS NECESSARY

Why do we have to be regenerated? There are two reasons which make it necessary. First, speaking from the lower aspect, regeneration is necessary because our life has been corrupted and become evil (Jer. 17:9; Rom. 7:18), and it cannot be changed from evil to good (Jer. 13:23). This is the reason we usually give for regeneration. Because our life (1) is corrupt and wicked, and (2) cannot be improved, we therefore need to be regenerated. All the sages of the past and present have advocated the doctrine of self-improvement in order to improve man. But God's salvation does not correct or improve man, but regenerates man, since our human life is already corrupted and cannot be made good by improvement. This is the first reason we must be regenerated.

Second, speaking from the higher aspect, there is another reason we need to be regenerated. But first, let us ask: If our life had not been corrupted and become evil, would we still need to be regenerated? Yes; we would still need to be regenerated, because our human life is only a created life, not God's uncreated life. When we were created, we obtained only created life; we did not obtain God's uncreated life. God's purpose for us human beings is that we may obtain His uncreated life and be transformed into His image to be like Him, as He is. Therefore, even if our human life had not been corrupted, we would still need to be regenerated.

In the beginning, although Adam's life was not corrupted, it was a created life, not an uncreated life; a human life, not God's life. Therefore, even if man had not fallen or his life had not been corrupted, even though he were good without any evil, he would still need regeneration. God's purpose in creating man is not only to obtain a good man, but even more to have a *GOD-man,* one who has God's life and nature and is just like God. If God desired man to be only a good man, and man had not fallen and been corrupted, he would not need to be regenerated. But God's desire is not that man should be only a good man, but, much more, a GOD-man, one who is the same as He is. Therefore, even a good man must be regenerated.

Do not take this second reason lightly. This is a very significant matter. Oh, the purpose of regeneration is that we may have God's life and be like God! It is needless to say that we are corrupted and evil and cannot be improved; but even if we were absolutely good or could be improved to become perfect, we would still need to be regenerated in order to possess God's life.

God created man with the aim that man may be like Him and be a GOD-man, possessing His life and nature. But when He created man, He did not put His life into man. He wanted man to exercise his own will to choose to receive His life. Therefore, even if we created human beings had not fallen, we would still need to obtain God's life in addition to our original human life. This means that we must be born again.

Therefore, the reasons for regeneration are of two aspects: The lower one is that our life is corrupt and evil and cannot be changed; therefore, we require another life by which we can live. The higher one is that it is God's intention that man be like Him; therefore, we must obtain God's life beside our own life. May we all see this so that henceforth, when we speak about regeneration, we will point out this higher aspect also, enabling people to see that even if we were perfect and sinless, we would still need to be regenerated.

II. WHAT IS REGENERATION?

According to the Scripture, to be regenerated is to be born of the Spirit (John 3:3-6). Originally our spirit was dead, but at the time we believed, God's Spirit came to touch our spirit; thus, our spirit obtained God's life and was made alive. It is in this way that God's Spirit gave birth to us, apart from our first, natural birth. In brief, to be regenerated is to be born once again, to be born of God (John 1:13), or, apart from our original human life to obtain God's life.

To be regenerated means to be born again. Why do we use the term "born again"? Originally we were born of our parents; but now we are born once more, this time of *God;* hence, this experience is called being born again. Being born of our parents caused us to obtain human life, whereas being born of God causes us to have God's life. Therefore, we who have been regenerated have God's life in addition to the human life.

Therefore, we must clearly see that to be regenerated is to be born of God, or, in addition to our original human life, to possess God's life. Apart from our original life, God puts His life into us—this is regeneration.

III. HOW CAN WE BE REGENERATED?

How can a man be regenerated? In brief, God's Spirit enters into man's spirit and puts God's life into it; thus, man becomes regenerated.

How can God's Spirit enter into man's spirit? When man hears the Gospel or reads the word of the Scripture, God's Spirit works in him and causes him to feel that he has sinned and is corrupted; hence, he is reproved for sin and righteousness and judgment (John 16:8). When man sees himself as a sinner, recognizes his corruption, and is willing to repent, then God's Spirit causes him to see that the Lord Jesus is his Savior, and that He died on the cross to shed His blood for the remission of sin. At this moment, he automatically believes in the Lord and receives Him as his Savior. Once he receives the

Lord as his Savior, God's Spirit enters into his spirit and puts God's life in it, causing him to be regenerated.

So, speaking from the standpoint of the Spirit of God, it is God's Spirit entering into our spirit to put God's life in it which causes us to be regenerated. From our standpoint it is because of our repenting, believing, and accepting the Lord Jesus as our Savior that we become regenerated, which means that in addition to our original life we obtain the life of God.

IV. THE RESULTS OF REGENERATION

The results or accomplishments of regeneration may be briefly categorized into three items:

1) Regeneration causes men to become the children of God. Since regeneration means to be born of God, it automatically causes men to become the children of God (John 1:12, 13) and have the relationship of life with God. The life which is obtained from God through regeneration enables men to be God's children; this life is also the authority for men to be God's children. Such children of God, having God's life and nature, and able to be just like God, can fulfill God's purpose in creating man.

2) Regeneration causes men to become a new creation. A new creation is that which has the elements of God within it. When something has God's elements within it, it is a new creation. In the old creation, there is no element of God. We human beings originally do not have any of God's elements; therefore, we are the old creation. It is not until God's element is added into us that we become the new creation. This is what regeneration has accomplished in us. Regeneration causes us to have God's life and His very element, thereby making us a new creation (2 Cor. 5:17). This new creation is the crystallization of God being mingled with man, and it is the most wonderful thing in the universe: it has both the human and divine elements, it is both man and God, and it is like both man and God.

3) Regeneration causes men to be united with God as one. It not only causes man to obtain God's life and His elements, but also to be united with God as one. By regeneration, God

the Spirit enters into man's spirit, causing man to be joined with Him as one spirit (1 Cor. 6:17). This is God causing man to have the deepest relationship with Himself, to become one with Himself.

In conclusion, when the Holy Spirit, by our believing in the Lord Jesus, puts God's life into our spirit and causes us to be born of God, to become God's children, and in the new creation to be united with God as one, this is regeneration.

CHAPTER FOUR

THAT WHICH IS GAINED
THROUGH REGENERATION

If we desire to seek growth in life, we must understand what regeneration is all about, and we must know what we have gained through regeneration. Regeneration affords us a beginning in life, and that which is gained through regeneration affords us the growth in life. Hence, if we want to seek growth in life, we should have some knowledge concerning regeneration, and we should know that which is gained through regeneration.

That which is gained through regeneration is very closely related to the results of regeneration. The results of regeneration issue from what is gained through regeneration, the former being accomplished because of the latter. The results of regeneration are that which regeneration accomplishes upon us, while that which is gained through regeneration are the things which we receive through regeneration. Because regeneration has caused us to gain certain things, it can have certain accomplishments upon us. Regeneration can make us children of God because regeneration causes us to gain the life of God. Regeneration can make us a new creation because it causes us to gain the elements of God. Regeneration can unite us with God because regeneration causes us to gain the Spirit of God. All the accomplishments of regeneration upon us are achieved because of the things we have obtained through regeneration. Not only do such things cause us to have various experiences in the spiritual life at the time of regeneration, but also after regeneration they cause us to grow in life. Hence if we are seeking to grow in life, we must know the things which we have gained through regeneration.

According to the teaching of the Bible, regeneration causes us to receive at least seven things. These seven things are either divine and great or very important and close to us. Let us look briefly at these seven things one by one.

I. THE LIFE OF GOD

The first thing we gain through regeneration is the life of God. We have already seen in the previous chapter that regeneration occurs when the Spirit of God puts the life of God into our spirit. In regeneration, the primary thing the Spirit of God does is to put the life of God into us. Therefore, the primary thing which regeneration gives us is the life of God.

But what is the life of God? It is the content of God and God Himself. All that is in God and all that God Himself is are in the life of God. All the fullness of the Godhead is hidden in the life of God. The nature of God is also contained in the life of God. Every facet of what God is, is included in the life of God.

With any kind of living thing, all that it is rests within its life. All of its capabilities and functions issue out of its life, and all of its outward activities and expressions originate from its life. It is that kind of living thing because it has that kind of life. Its being rests in its life. This is an evident principle.

God is the supreme living being, and all that He is, of course (and even more so), is in His life. All that He is—whether truth, holiness, light or love—is derived from His life. All His expressions—whether goodness, righteousness, kindness, or forgiveness—are derived from His life. His life causes Him to have such divine capabilities and functions inwardly and such divine actions and expressions outwardly as well. The reason He is such a God is that He has such a life. Hence His being God rests in His life.

Because the life of God is the content of God, in it is hidden the fullness of God, and in it is contained the nature of God Himself; therefore, when we receive the life of God, we receive the fullness of God (Col. 2:9-10), and we have the nature of God (2 Pet. 1:3-4). Because all that God has in

Himself and all that God Himself is rests in the life of God, when we receive this life, we receive all that God has in Himself and all that God Himself is. Because the life of God causes God to have such divine capabilities and functions within Him, the life of God in us can also cause us to have the same kind of capabilities and functions in us as in God. Because all that God is and does comes from His life, this life in us can also cause us to be what God is and do what God does, which means it can cause us to be like God and to live out God.

Brothers and sisters, have you ever realized that because the life of God is in us we have all the capabilities and functions in us which are in God? Have you ever realized that because we have the life of God in us we can be what God is and do what God does? In God there is the capability of holiness and the function of light. Because the life of God is in us, the same capability of holiness and function of light are in us as in God. Just as God can live out His holiness and shine forth His light from Himself, so also we, because of the life of God within us, can live out His holiness and shine forth His light from us, which means we can be holy as God is holy and shining as God is shining. What God is, is love, and what God does is righteousness. Since we have the life of God in us, we can be what God is and do what God does. Even as God can be love and do righteousness, so also we, because of the life of God in us, can be the love that God is and do the righteousness that God does. This means that we can love as God loves and be righteous as God is righteous. Thus, we can be like God and live out God.

We should further know that the life of God is that great power which resurrected the Lord Jesus. When the Lord Jesus was resurrected, He cast off death and overcame death. Death is very strong (S. S. 8:6). In the whole universe, besides God and the life of God, there is nothing which is stronger than death. When the Lord Jesus entered into death, death used all its power to hold the Lord, but the Lord broke through the holding power of death and arose! The Lord can thus arise and not be held by death (Acts 2:24) because there is in Him the powerful life of God. It was the life of God's great power which enabled Him to break through the mighty holding power of death. The life of God which regeneration gives us is this great powerful life of God! This great powerful life of God is the great power of resurrection in us today which enables us to cast off death and overcome all that belongs to death, just as God overcame them.

The Bible shows us that God has two kinds of great power: one is the great power of creation; the other is the great power of resurrection. God's mighty power of creation calls into being that which does not exist. The great power of resurrection gives life to the dead. This is what Abraham believed (Rom. 4:17). God's great power of creation, resting in the hand of God, is able to create all things for man. God's great power of resurrection, resting in the life of God and being the life of God, enables man to be delivered from all the dead things which are outside of God, and thus live out God Himself. Oh, the life of God we receive through regeneration is this great resurrection power of God! Through regeneration, God has wrought His life into us, which means He has wrought His great resurrection power into us. Oh, may we see that this life of God, which we receive when we are regenerated, is God's great power of resurrection! This life which is in us today can make us as strong as God is. Just as God is able to overcome death, so we also are able to overcome death because of this life of great power within us. What a life this life of God is which we obtained through regeneration! To what an extent this life can make us like God! How we should worship and thank God for this life!

II. THE LAW OF LIFE

Since regeneration gives us the life of God, it also gives us the law of life. Because the life of God entered into us, the law of life which is contained in this life was brought into us too.

Every kind of life has its own innate ability, which is its natural function. And the natural function of every kind of life is its natural law or its law of life. When a certain life gets into, a certain creature, it causes that creature to have its natural law or its law of life. Likewise, the life of God has its divine ability, which is its divine natural functions. And the natural functions of God's life are its natural law or the law of life. When the life of God enters into us, it brings into us the natural law contained in it, and this law becomes the law of life within us. Thus, when the life of God enters into us, the law of life contained in it also enters into us. Since the life of God is something which we have gained through regeneration, the law of life which it brings with it was also gained through regeneration.

We have seen in chapter one that in the life of God is contained the nature of God, and in the life of God is hidden the fullness of God; therefore, the law contained in the life of God is compatible with God Himself, with what God is, and with the nature of God; hence, this law is the law of God Himself. When the life of God brings its law into us, this also means that it brings the law of God into us.

The law of life which the life of God brings into us are the laws mentioned in Hebrews 8:10, which God put into our minds and wrote in our hearts. These laws are different from the laws of the Old Testament. The laws of the Old Testament are the laws of God which God had written with characters on stone tablets outside of man (Exo. 34:1, 28). The laws of life are the laws of God which God has written with His life on our heart-tablet within us. The laws which were written on the stone tablets are outward laws, laws of letter, dead laws, and laws without power; they are laws which are unable to accomplish anything upon man (Rom. 8:3; Heb. 7:18-19). The laws which are written on the tablet of our heart are inward laws, the laws of life, living laws, and laws with great power; they enable us not only to know the heart desire of God and follow His will, but also to know God Himself and live out God Himself.

The natural laws contained in any kind of life always cause the creature to know spontaneously how to live and how to act; thus, they become the living laws within that creature. Take the example of a hen: how she should live and how she should lay eggs are the natural laws contained in the hen's life; they make her know spontaneously how to do these things and thus live them out. Man need not give her any law from without. The natural laws contained in the life which is in her are the living laws within her. They spontaneously make her know that she should live in this way, and they enable her to live in this way.

Likewise, the natural laws contained in the life of God in us are its natural abilities; they enable us to know spontaneously how God would want us to act and behave, how to be pleasing to Him and how we may live out Himself. Whether anything agrees with the nature of God or contradicts the nature of God, whether it is something God wants us to do or something He does not want us to do, the natural abilities or the natural laws of the life of God cause us to know this, give us a sense of this. Thus, the natural abilities or the natural laws of the life of God become our inward laws.

Because these laws which are written in us are the natural abilities and natural laws of the life of God, the Bible calls them the "law." "The law of the Spirit of life" mentioned in Romans 8:2 is this law of life that is in us. Because this law is derived from the life of God, and the life of God rests in the Spirit of God and cannot be separated from the Spirit of God, Romans 8 names this law "the law of the Spirit of life." The life of God is in the Spirit of God and joined to the Spirit of God; the Spirit of God contains the life of God; it is the Spirit of the life of God. Since this law is derived from the life of God, it is therefore from the Spirit of the life of God. Since it is the law of the life of God, it is also the law of the Spirit of the life of God.

The life of God is powerful; the Spirit of God is also powerful. The law of the Spirit of life, derived from the powerful life of God and the powerful Spirit of God, is also powerful. We may say that the life of God in us is the source of this law, and the Spirit of God in us is the executor of this law. Thus, this law in us is especially strong and mighty; not only does it enable us to have divine knowledge, it also enables us to have divine power. Once we are regenerated and have the life of God, God wants us to be His people and live in Him according to this strong and mighty law, this law of great power. After we are saved, God wants us to live in His life and live out His life as well according to this law in us, this law of life, this living law.

III. A NEW HEART

Ezekiel 36:26 tells us that when God cleanses us, saves us, or regenerates us, He gives us a new heart. Thus, according to the teaching of the Bible, regeneration also gives us a new heart.

What is a new heart? A new heart means that the old heart has become new; the new heart comes from the renewing of our old heart. For God to give us a new heart means that God renews our old heart. After Ezekiel 36:26 says that God gives us a new heart, it says that He takes away our stony heart and gives us a heart of flesh. From this verse, it is clear that God gives us a new heart by renewing our old heart.

Originally our heart opposed God, did not desire God, and was as hard as stone toward God; thus, it became a "stony heart." When the Holy Spirit regenerates us, He causes our heart to repent of sin and become soft toward God. Hence, after regeneration, our stony heart becomes a "heart of flesh." That hard stony heart is the old heart we had; this soft heart of flesh is the new heart God gives us. This means that when we are regenerated, God renews our old heart and makes it soft.

Our heart is the organ of our inclination and affection toward things; it represents us with regard to our inclination, affection, delight, and desire toward things. All our inclination, affection, delight, and desire are functions of our heart. Before we were regenerated, our heart was inclined toward sin, loved the world, and desired the things of passion; toward God, however, it was cold and hard, without inclination and without affection; toward the things of God and spiritual things, it had no delight and was void of any desire. So when God regenerates us, He renews our heart and makes our heart a new heart, with a new inclination, new affection, new delight, and new desire. Thus, once we are regenerated and saved, our heart inclines toward God, loves God, and desires God; toward the things of God, the spiritual things, and the heavenly things, it also has delight and desire. Whenever such things are mentioned, our heart is joyful, responsive, and desirous.

Brothers and sisters, have you seen this? The reason that God renews our heart and gives us a new heart at the time of our regeneration is that He wants us to incline toward Him, adore Him, desire Him, and love Him. Before, we did not love Him and we could not love Him, because our heart was old and hard. Now He has renewed, softened, and turned our heart; thus, we are both able and willing to love Him. Since our heart by being renewed has become a new heart, it now has a new function. This new function is that it can incline toward God and love God and the things of God.

Since regeneration gives us a new heart, it causes us to have a new inclination and love, a new desire and longing. This new inclination, love, desire, and longing are all toward God and the things of God. This is the function of the new heart; this is also the purpose of God in giving us a new heart.

IV. A NEW SPIRIT

After Ezekiel 36:26 says that God gives us a new heart, it says that God also puts a new spirit in us. Thus, not only does regeneration cause us to have a new heart; it also causes us to have a new spirit.

What is a new spirit? A new spirit means that our dead old spirit has been renewed and quickened. Just as the new heart is the old heart made new, so the new spirit is the old spirit made new. The old heart, when it is renewed, is softened; while the old spirit, when it is renewed, is quickened. This is because the trouble with our old heart is its hardness, whereas the trouble with our old spirit is its deadness. There-fore, when God regenerates us, just as He renews our hard old heart by softening it to become a new heart, so He renews our dead old spirit by quickening it to become a new spirit.

The created spirit of man originally was the organ for man to contact God. Man had fellowship with God and communed with God through and by his spirit. Later, because of man's fall, his spirit was damaged by the defilement of sin. Thus, the human spirit lost its function toward God and became a dead spirit. Because it was dead, it was therefore old. When we are regenerated, because the blood of the Lord Jesus cleanses the defilement which our spirit suffered, the Spirit of God then puts the life of God, which is the element of God, into our spirit and quickens it (see Col. 2:13). In this way, our dead old spirit is renewed and becomes a living new spirit.

Our spirit originally was an old creation; there was no element of God in it. Later, not only did it have no element of God, but it was further defiled by sin; thus, it became old. There are two reasons for anything being a part of the old creation: one is that it was without the element of God during creation; the other is that it is defiled and corrupted by sin and Satan. It is also due to these two reasons that our spirit became an old spirit. Hence, when God regenerates us, in order to renew our old spirit and make it a new spirit, He works from two sides. On one hand, He uses the blood of the Lord Jesus to cleanse away the defilement of our spirit, so that our spirit becomes clean. On the other hand, He uses His Spirit to put His life into our spirit, so that our spirit may have His element. Thus, He renews our old spirit and makes it a new spirit. His renewing of our old spirit and making it a new spirit means that He puts a new spirit in us.

Since at the time of our regeneration God has already given us a new heart, why does He proceed further and put a new spirit in us? It is because the heart can only desire God and love God; it cannot contact God or touch God. Therefore, it is not sufficient for God to give us only a new heart; He must also put a new spirit in us. If God only gives us a new heart, He can only cause us to desire Him and love Him; He cannot enable us to contact Him. Therefore, He must put a new spirit in us so that we may contact Him and fellowship with Him.

We have already mentioned that the heart is the organ of our inclination and love. Therefore, the function of the heart toward God is to incline toward Him and love Him. The Bible says that the heart pants after God, the heart thirsts for God (Psa. 42:1-2). The heart can pant after God and thirst after God, but it cannot contact God or touch God. The heart has only the function of loving God and thirsting for Him; it does not have the ability to contact God or touch God. That which can contact God is not the heart, but the spirit. The heart is only good for us to love God, but the spirit is good for us to contact God and to fellowship with God.

For example, suppose I have here a good pen. My heart likes it very much; but my heart cannot contact it or take possession of it, for my heart does not have such ability. Such ability belongs to my hand. The hand illustrates the spirit. Although our heart loves God and thirsts deeply for Him, it can neither contact God nor fellowship with Him. Only our spirit can do that. Therefore, when we are regenerated, God not only gives us a new heart, He also puts a new spirit within us.

With a new heart, we can desire God and love God, and with a new spirit we can contact God and touch God. Our new heart enables us to have new delight and inclinations, new feelings and interest toward God and the things of God. Our new spirit enables us to have new contact and insight, new spiritual ability and function toward God and the things of God. Formerly, we neither loved God nor liked the spiritual things of God; moreover, we were not able to contact God or understand the spiritual things of God. But now we have a new heart and a new spirit; therefore, we not only can love God and the things of God, we can also contact God and know God and the things of God. Formerly, we had no feeling toward God and no interest in God; we were weak and without any ability whatsoever toward God and the things of God. But now, with a new heart and a new spirit, we not only have feeling and interest toward God and the things of God, but we also are strongly able to contact and understand them. Hence, once our heart loves God, our spirit touches Him; once our heart delights in the things of God, our spirit understands them. This is the intention of God in giving us a new spirit in addition to a new heart.

V. THE HOLY SPIRIT

After Ezekiel 36:26 says that God gives us a new heart and puts within us a new spirit, verse 27 goes on to say that God puts His own Spirit within us. Therefore, among the things which we gain through regeneration, there is also the Spirit of God.

Originally, we did not have the Spirit of God. And not only did we not have the Spirit of God, but our own spirit was dead toward God. When God regenerated us, on one hand He caused His Spirit to put His life into our spirit, thus quickening our dead spirit; and on the other hand, God also put His Spirit into our spirit, which means that He caused His Spirit to dwell in our quickened, new spirit. Thus, within us who are regenerated, there is not only a quickened, new spirit, which has the element of God's life, but also the Spirit of God dwelling in our new spirit.*

Why does God put His Spirit within us? What is the function of God's Spirit dwelling in our spirit? According to the Bible, there are at least seven aspects of the main functions of the Spirit of God dwelling within us:

A. As the Indwelling Spirit

God puts His Spirit in us so that His Spirit may be the indwelling Spirit within us, that we may know God and experience all that God in Christ has accomplished for us (Rom. 8:9-11). This is the special blessing given by God in the New Testament era; it did not exist in the Old Testament. In the Old Testament, God only caused His Spirit to come from without to work upon man; He did not cause His Spirit to dwell *within* man. Only after the Lord's death and resurrection did God give His Spirit to us and cause His Spirit to dwell in us as the indwelling Spirit (John 14:16-17). Thus, He is able to reveal both God and Christ to us from within, that we in Christ may receive and enjoy the fullness of God (Col. 2:9-10).

B. As the Comforter

The Lord told us of the Comforter in John 14:16-17. He said that He would pray the Father to give us the Holy Spirit to dwell in us as another Comforter. This word "Comforter" in

---

* Romans 8:9 says, "The Spirit of God dwelleth in you," and verse 16 says, "The Spirit himself beareth witness with our spirit." From these two verses we see that the Spirit of God dwelling in us means that He dwells in our spirit; He is with our spirit.

the original text is the same as the word "Advocate" in 1 John 2:1, which when transliterated is "Paraclete," or "an advocate by the side." Originally, God gave His Son to be our Comforter, to be our Paraclete. When His Son returned to Him, He then gave His Spirit to us to be another Comforter, another Paraclete. This also means that He sent His Spirit as the embodiment of His Son to be our Comforter. Therefore, the Spirit of God dwelling in us is the very embodiment of Christ within us. He takes care of us from within, being fully responsible for us, just as Christ is for us before God.

C. As the Spirit of Truth

In John 14:16-17 the Lord tells us that the Holy Spirit who comes to dwell in us as the Comforter is "the Spirit of truth." Hence, the Spirit of God dwelling in us is also the Spirit of truth. The word truth in the original text means reality. Therefore, the Spirit of God, who dwells in us as "the Spirit of truth" or "the Spirit of reality," causes all that God and Christ are to be reality within us. All that God is and all that He in Christ has prepared for us, and all that Christ is and all that He by His death and resurrection has accomplished for us, are revealed and imparted to us as reality by this Spirit of God who dwells in us. Thus, we may touch and experience them so that they become ours.

D. As the Spirit of Life

Romans 8 calls the Holy Spirit who dwells in us the "Spirit of life" (vv. 9, 2). This shows us that the Spirit of God who dwells in us is also the Spirit of the life of God. Although the life of God is in Christ (John 1:4), yet it is known and experienced by us through the Holy Spirit who dwells within us. All the matters which relate to life are made known to us by this Holy Spirit who dwells in us. All experiences of life are also made ours by this Holy Spirit who dwells in us.

E. As the Seal

Ephesians 1:13 and 4:30 show us that the Holy Spirit we receive at regeneration is within us as the seal. When God puts His Spirit in us, it means that He stamps His Spirit upon us as a seal. When a seal is stamped on an article, it not only becomes a sign of ownership on that thing, but it also makes an impression upon that article just as a stamp used for sealing. This is the function of the Spirit of God in us as the seal. The Spirit of God dwelling in us not only serves as a mark, showing that we belong to God and marking us out from amidst the men of the world, but furthermore, as the embodiment of God and Christ, He seals us according to the image of God and Christ so that we become like God, like Christ.

F. As the Earnest

Ephesians 1:14 and 2 Corinthians 1:22 tell us that the Holy Spirit of God dwells in us as the earnest. An earnest is a pledge or a guarantee. The Spirit of God dwelling in us is not only a seal, marking us out as belonging to God and sealing us after the image of God; He is also the earnest, guaranteeing that God and all things which are of God are our portion and inheritance to be enjoyed.

G. As the Anointing

First John 2:27 says that within us there is the "anointing" which we have received of the Lord. Anointing in the Bible refers to the Spirit of God (Luke 4:18). Therefore, this verse tells us that the Spirit of God dwelling in us is the anointing. This anointing in us often anoints us. The anointing is the moving of the Spirit of God within us. The Spirit of God moving in us or anointing us means that He anoints God Himself into us, that the element of God may become our inward element, and that we may know God and His desire and will in everything.*

How high and glorious these seven functions are! Not only do they show us the functions of the Spirit of God dwelling in us, but they make known to us what a Spirit this Spirit of God is which we have received through regeneration.

---

* A detailed explanation of this point is given in the book *The Experience of Life* (published by the Living Stream Ministry), chapter seven.

VI. CHRIST

Romans 8:9-10 shows us that the Spirit of God dwelling in us is the Spirit of Christ dwelling in us; and the Spirit of Christ dwelling in us is Christ dwelling in us. This reveals that the Spirit of God in us is the embodiment of Christ. Since regeneration causes us to have the Spirit of God within us, it also causes us to have Christ within us.

When we believe, God through His Spirit reveals Christ in us (Gal. 1:16). Therefore, once we receive Christ as Savior, He as the Spirit dwells in us (2 Cor. 13:5).

What is the purpose of Christ dwelling in us? It is that He may be our life. Although Christ dwells in us to be our all, the central reason for His indwelling is that He might be our life.

God in His salvation has regenerated us that we might receive His life, have His nature, and thereby be entirely like Him. He puts His life in Christ for us to receive (John 1:4; 1 John 5:11, 12). In other words, He wants Christ to be our life (John 14:6; Col. 3:4). Although it is His Spirit who puts His life in us, and although it is His Spirit who enables us to know, experience, and live out His life, yet His life is Christ. Although through His Spirit He causes us to receive, know, and experience His life, yet He makes Christ our life. God through His Spirit revealing Christ in us means that He wants Christ to be our life. Christ dwelling in us means that He lives in us as our life (Gal. 2:20) and wants to live out His life from us (2 Cor. 4:10-11). Thus, He wants us, in His life, to grow into His image and become like Him (2 Cor. 3:18). When we, in His life, grow into His image and become like Him, we grow into the image of God and become like God, because He is the image of God (Col. 1:15).

We have already seen that the life of God is all that God is; therefore, when God puts His life in Christ, He puts all that He is in Christ. Christ is the incarnation of God, the embodiment of God. All that God is and all the fullness of the Godhead dwell in Christ bodily (Col. 2:9). Therefore, Christ dwelling in us causes us to be filled with all the fullness of God (Eph. 3:17-19).

Christ dwelling in us as our life enables us not only to

enjoy all the fullness of God today, but also to enter into
the glory of God in the future (Rom. 8:17; Heb. 2:10). Therefore, dwelling in us today, He is on one hand our life, and on
the other hand He is our hope of glory (Col. 3:4; 1:27). His
dwelling in us as our life today means that, through the life of
God in Him, He will cause us to grow and become like God, to
grow and be conformed to the image of God, and eventually
to grow into the glory of God.

VII. GOD

Christ is the embodiment of God. Since regeneration
causes us to obtain Christ, it also causes us to have God. Furthermore, Christ is the embodiment of God, and the Holy
Spirit is the reality of Christ. God is in Christ, and Christ is
the Holy Spirit. Therefore, when regeneration causes us to
have the Holy Spirit, it causes us not only to have Christ, but
also to have God.

Ever since God regenerated us, He in Christ through His
Spirit has been dwelling in us. The apostle John says that we
know God dwells in us by the Holy Spirit which He has given
us (1 John 3:24; 4:13). The Lord Jesus also says that He and
God together abide in us (John 14:23). Therefore, whether it
is the Holy Spirit or Christ dwelling in us, it is God dwelling
in us. God is in Christ, and Christ is the Spirit. Therefore, the
Spirit dwelling in us is Christ dwelling in us; and Christ
dwelling in us is God dwelling in us. God is in Christ dwelling
in us, and Christ is the Spirit dwelling in us. Therefore, when
we have the Spirit dwelling in us, we have Christ and God
dwelling in us. The Spirit, Christ, and God—all three—dwell
in us as one, which means the Triune God is dwelling in us.

But when the Bible mentions the Holy Spirit dwelling in
us, the emphasis is on His anointing in us (1 John 2:27); when
it mentions Christ dwelling in us, the emphasis is on His
living in us as our life (Gal. 2:20); and when it mentions
God dwelling in us, the emphasis is on His working in us
(Phil. 2:13; Heb. 13:21; 1 Cor. 12:6). The Bible gives very
clear distinctions concerning these three matters. Concerning
the Holy Spirit dwelling in us, it speaks of "anointing";
concerning Christ dwelling in us, it speaks of "living"; and

concerning God dwelling in us, it speaks of "working." It never says that Christ or God is anointing us, that the Holy Spirit or God is living in us, or that the Holy Spirit or Christ is working in us. It only says that the Holy Spirit anoints us, Christ lives in us, and God works in us. These three manners of speaking are not interchangeable. "Anointing" is related to the Holy Spirit as the ointment in us; "living" is related to Christ being life in us, and "working" is related to God working in us.

The Holy Spirit dwelling in us is as ointment; therefore, what He does in us is to anoint. Christ dwelling in us is as life; therefore, what He does in us is to live. God dwelling in us is a matter of working; therefore, what He does in us is to work. The Holy Spirit, by anointing us, anoints the element of God into us. Christ, by living in us, lives the life of God both in us and out from us. God, by working in us, works His will into us that it may be accomplished upon us.

Therefore, we must see that what we obtain through regeneration is too great, too high, too rich, and too glorious. Through regeneration we obtain the life of God and the law of this life. Through regeneration we obtain a new heart and a new spirit. Through regeneration we further obtain the Holy Spirit, Christ, and God Himself. These are truly sufficient for us—sufficient to make us holy and spiritual, sufficient to make us victorious and transcendent, and sufficient to make us grow and mature in life.

CHAPTER FIVE

THE SENSE OF LIFE

We have seen what life is and what the experience of life is. We have also seen the first experience of life, which is regeneration, and the various things which are gained through regeneration. Now that we have seen these, we can come to the matter of the sense of life.

The sense of life, as far as we are concerned, is very subjective, personal, and practical. Therefore, if we are to have any pursuit in life, we must pay attention to this sense of life and know it well. All those who have the experience of life know the deep relationship which exists between the sense of life and the experience of life. Therefore, if we would investigate the subject of the knowledge of life, we must look into the matter of the sense of life.

I. THE SCRIPTURAL BASIS

Although the Bible does not mention explicitly the sense of life, yet it actually speaks of the matter. Romans 8:6 says, "For the mind of the flesh is death; but the mind of the Spirit is life and peace." This verse speaks to us very clearly concerning the sense of life, for the peace mentioned here is clearly a matter of consciousness. This peace does not refer to the outward environment, but the inward condition; therefore, it is definitely a matter of feeling. Since the peace mentioned here is a matter of feeling, the death and life mentioned here are also a matter of feeling.

The sense of death causes us to sense the element of death. The elements of death are: weakness, emptiness, depression, darkness, and pain. Death includes at least these five elements, and the sum total of these elements is largely equivalent to death. Death causes men to become weak; and when men become extremely weak, they die. Death causes men to become empty, because death ends everything. Death causes men to become depressed and down-hearted; the most depressed and silent ones are the dead ones. Death also darkens men; those in deepest darkness are those who have entered into death. At the same time, death causes men to suffer pain; one who suffers the most pain is one who has fallen into death. All these are the elements of death; therefore, when we sense these, we sense death.

These senses of death are results of our minding the flesh. Whenever we mind the flesh, we will immediately have these feelings of death. For example, if on the Lord's day you mind the flesh a little in the afternoon, when you come to the breaking of bread meeting in the evening you will feel weak inside and unable to rise up. At the same time, you will feel empty, depressed, and perhaps even dark and in pain. All these feelings are the senses of death. Sometimes you sense one stronger than the other; sometimes you sense them all evenly. Nevertheless, it is due to our minding the flesh that we sense death.

The sense of life is just the opposite of the sense of death. The sense of death makes us feel weak and empty, whereas the sense of life makes us feel strong and satisfied. The sense of death makes us feel depressed, dark, and in pain. The sense of life makes us feel lively, bright, and comfortable. Because the sense of life makes us feel strong, satisfied, lively, bright, and comfortable, it causes us also to have the sense of peace, that is, to feel good and at ease.

We should realize that the things mentioned in Romans 8:6 are all in contrast with each other. The flesh is in contrast with the spirit, and death is in contrast with life and peace. The opposite of death is not only life, but also peace. Therefore, death includes not only weakness, emptiness, depression, and darkness, but it also includes pain. Weakness, emptiness, depression, and darkness are in contrast with life, while pain is in contrast with peace.

The sense of death is due to our minding the flesh, while the sense of life and peace is due to our minding the spirit. When we live in the spirit, follow the spirit, and mind the spirit, we feel strong and satisfied within; at the same time we also feel lively, bright, comfortable, and at ease. For example, if the Holy Spirit gives you a feeling, and you mind and obey it, you will feel strong and satisfied within; at the same time you will feel lively, bright, comfortable, and at ease. Thus, you will have the feeling of life and peace, because you mind the spirit.

The reason Romans 8:6 mentions the sense of life is that it has mentioned three things previously: the Spirit, life, and the law of life. The Spirit is in us and becomes one spirit with our spirit: life is included in the Spirit as the content of the Spirit; and the law is the natural ability and function of life. These three joined together become the law of the Spirit of life, which is responsible in us for all matters of life, giving us a certain sense anytime and anywhere. Whenever we mind the spirit and act and live according to the spirit, this law gives us the feeling of life and peace. To sense life is to feel strong, satisfied, lively, bright, and fresh. To sense peace is to feel comfortable, at ease, good, and natural. If we mind the flesh and act and live according to the flesh, this law will give us the sense of death, that is, we will feel weak, empty, depressed, dark, and in pain.

Therefore, what Romans 8:6 speaks of is wholly a matter of consciousness, and this consciousness is given to us by the law of the Spirit of life. Since the law of the Spirit of life belongs to life, the consciousness that it gives also belongs to life. Therefore, since the consciousness mentioned in Romans 8:6 is given to us by this law, it belongs to the sense of life.

The second place in the Scripture concerning the matter of the sense of life is in Ephesians 4:19, which says that the Gentiles "being past feeling gave themselves up to lasciviousness, to work all uncleanness with greediness." This tells us that the reason the people in the world commit sin and do wickedness at will is that they have forsaken all feelings. Indeed, when man sins and does wickedness, he must have already forsaken the feelings within him. When a man sins and does wickedness, we cannot say that he has no feeling, but at least we can say that he has laid aside his feelings. If one does not lay aside the feelings, if one is restricted by the inner feelings, do you think he can still commit sin and do wickedness? All who sin and do wickedness are those who have laid aside their feelings. Anyone who commits sin and does wickedness must lay aside his feelings. When anyone cheats, steals, beats others, robs others, or does any other bad and evil deeds, he must lay aside his feelings. The more one commits sin and does wickedness, the more he must lay aside the inner consciousness. Therefore, an evil, wicked man is void of feelings, whereas a good and kind person is rich in feeling.

Now, whose inner sense is stronger, the Christian's or the Gentile's? If we compare the Christians and the unbelievers, is our consciousness stronger, or is theirs? We must answer that our feelings are much stronger, because, in addition to the feelings they have, we have the feelings of life within us, which they do not have. Therefore, if we sin and commit wickedness, we must have laid aside our feelings even more severely than they. For this very reason, the Scripture exhorts us not to cast aside all feelings as do the Gentiles. The Scripture thus beseeches us that we might take care of our inner sense. This of course emphasizes heeding the inner sense of life. After Ephesians 4 exhorts us not to be like the unbelievers who cast aside all feelings, it goes on to say that we are to put off the old man and put on the new man. This new man belongs to the life in the Spirit. In order to live in this new man, we must live in the life which is in the Spirit. Therefore, Ephesians 4 exhorts us not to forsake all feelings as the unbelievers do, but to live in this new man. This means that we must live in the life which is in the Spirit, take care of the sense of life in the Spirit, and live according to this sense of life.

Furthermore, almost all the Epistles of the apostles have words of blessing and greeting in which grace and peace are mentioned. Grace is God gained by us, and peace is the feeling of having gained God. God gained by us to become our life and for us to enjoy is grace. This grace within us results in peace; it causes us to have a feeling of peacefulness within. A person who experiences God, enjoys the life of God, and tastes the power of the life of God daily is bound to have peace within him. This peace is the feeling he has when he enjoys grace. Therefore, if we do not have peace within, or we do not quite feel the peace, it proves that we are short of grace. When we are short of grace, it means that we are short of God. Since we have not gained God sufficiently within us, have not obtained enough supply of the life of God, and have not sufficiently experienced the power of the life of God, we are short of peace within. If we have gained enough of God within us and have experienced God and the life of God sufficiently, we will have enough peace within. This peace is not peace in the environment, but a condition of peace within. We must believe that the peace mentioned in the greetings of the apostles is this kind of inner peace. Inner peace is a matter of consciousness. When the apostles wished that the people might have peace, it means that they wished the people might have the peace of the inner sense, or peace within. The inner sense of peace is the sense of life. Therefore, when they expressed their wish that the people might have the feeling of peace within, they wanted them to pay attention to the inner sense of life.

II. THE SOURCE OF THE SENSE OF LIFE

Where does the sense of life we are speaking of come from? From what is it produced? It is produced from the things we have gained through regeneration—the life of God, the law of life, the Holy Spirit, Christ, and God. The life of God, the law of life, the Holy Spirit, Christ, and God cause us to have a feeling within, and this feeling is what we call the sense of life.

Every life has its feelings. Furthermore, the stronger the life is, the keener its feelings are. The life of God is the strongest life; therefore, when this life is in us it causes us not merely to have feelings, but to have strong feelings.

Since the law of life is derived from life, it also has feelings. Therefore, this law which is in us causes us to have feelings, especially when we disobey it. For example, when our body is normal, there is hardly any special feeling. But when it becomes sick there is strong feeling, and this strong feeling occurs when we disobey the law which is within the body. Similarly, when we obey the law of life, it does not give us much feeling, but when we disobey it, it gives very distinct feelings.

The Holy Spirit as ointment is anointing and moving in us; Christ is living in us with activity; and God is working in us. All three are in us with activity and action. They are not quiet and motionless; therefore, they all cause us to have feelings.

Thus, whether it be the life of God, the law of life, or the Holy Spirit, Christ, and God within us, they all cause us to have feelings. And they are mingled together in giving us feelings. Therefore, the feelings derived from all five are not five kinds of feelings, but one feeling, that is, the sense of life which we are speaking of.

Why is it that the feelings derived from these five—the life of God, the law of life, the Holy Spirit, Christ, and God—are just one kind of feeling? And why is this feeling the sense of life? It is because the Holy Spirit, Christ, and God are the Triune God; the life of God is God Himself; and the law of life comes out from this life of God. Therefore, strictly speaking, these five are one. Therefore, when they are in us, the feelings they give us are of one kind. The reason that this feeling is the feeling of life is that it is derived from the Triune God of life, the life of God, and the law of life. The main purpose of the Triune God in us is to be our life, and this life includes the law of life. Therefore, the feelings which they cause us to have are derived from life and belong to life; hence, they are the sense of life. This sense is one, but it has five aspects. It is derived from the life of God, and it is derived from the law of the life of God; therefore, it has the nature of the life of God and the function of the law of God's life as well. At the same time, this sense is also derived from the Holy Spirit, Christ, and God; therefore, it contains the element of the Holy Spirit anointing in us, the element of Christ living in us, and the element of God working and accomplishing His will in us. Because of these various aspects, this sense is rich, strong and keen; it is even richer, stronger, and keener than the best sense among the unbelievers. The best feelings that unbelievers can have are but the created sense of goodness in human beings. But besides the created sense of goodness, this sense of life is a divine sense added into us by the things which we have gained through regeneration.

III. THE FUNCTION OF THE SENSE OF LIFE

What then is the function or use of this sense of life? The function or use of the sense of life is to let us know continuously where we are living. Are we living in the natural life or in the life of the Spirit? Are we living in the flesh or in the spirit? This is what the sense of life makes known to us continuously, and it is for this that we have the sense of life. Therefore, the sense of life in us guides and proves us. If we follow the sense of life, we follow the guidance God gives us, and at the same time, we receive a verification of where we are living.

Now we shall apply what we have said. The sense of death makes known to us that we are not living in the spirit but in the flesh. Once we have the sense of death, we should know that we are not in the spirit but in the flesh. The sense of death includes weakness, emptiness, depression, darkness, and pain. Once we have such feelings, it means the sense of life in us is making known that we are already not right, that we are already not living in the spirit, but in the flesh.

Then, what feeling does the sense of life give so that we know we are right before God and living in the spirit? It gives us the feeling of life and peace, or, in other words, it makes us feel strong, satisfied, lively, bright, and comfortable. Whenever we feel strong, satisfied, lively, bright, and comfortable within, we have inward proof that we are right before God and that we are living in the spirit.

Therefore, the sense of life within us has a great function. It is there continuously leading us, making known to us where we should live; and it continuously proves to us where we are now living. It is this sense which leads us on in life; it is also this sense which continuously proves and reveals to us our real condition in life. Hence, it is our guide and testimony within. Whenever it causes us to feel inward life and peace, it proves that we have no problem in life. Whenever it makes us feel void of life and peace, it proves we have some problem in life.

You may say that you do not have the sense of life and peace within you, and neither do you have the sense of no life or no peace; you do not have the sense of being strong, satisfied, lively, bright, or comfortable, and neither do you have the sense of not being strong, satisfied, lively, bright, or comfortable. To be in such a condition proves you have a problem. We must positively have the sense of life and peace. We must feel strong, satisfied, lively, bright, comfortable, and at ease within; then all is well. Although at times, God wants to lead us out of our feelings and cause us to enter, as it were, into a cave, yet even in the cave we still have the sense of life and peace in our deepest part. Although the outward feelings are gone, there is still the feeling of life and peace in the deepest part.

Life and peace are the positive feelings which the sense of life gives us within, thus proving that our condition in life is normal. Weakness and uneasiness are the negative feelings which the sense of life gives us within, thus proving that we have some problem in life. The feelings both of weakness and uneasiness are the sense of death. The sense of death definitely comes from minding the flesh and touching anything outside of God. Every sense of death proves that we are more or less minding the flesh, and that we have touched to some extent the things outside of God. Therefore, whether we are minding the flesh, whether we are living in the spirit, and whether we are touching God, all depends upon the life and peace or weakness and uneasiness within us. If there is life and peace within, it proves that we are living in the spirit, we are touching God. If we feel weak and uneasy within, it proves that we are fleshly minded and are touching things outside of God.

It is not necessary that a Christian should never feel weak, but even when he feels weak, he should still feel strong. He feels weak because he has come to know himself; he feels strong because he touches Christ and knows Christ as his life. If we continually feel only weakness and never feel strong, something is wrong. The apostle said that whenever he is weak, then he is strong (2 Cor. 12:10). A strong person, even though he feels his own weakness, does not mind that weakness. If we always mind our weakness and cannot be strong, it proves we have a problem. It may be that we are more or less in the flesh, for weakness is a sense of death, and the sense of death always comes from minding the flesh.

A Christian can be weak yet feel strong; he can feel pain yet have the sense of peace. He feels pain because he meets tribulation from without; he has the sense of peace because he meets the Lord and touches the Lord from within. If we meet tribulation from without, yet inwardly we have no peace, something is wrong. The Lord says that in the world we have tribulation, but in Him we have peace (John 16:33). One who lives in the Lord, or one who lives in the spirit, may meet much tribulation from without, yet inwardly he still has peace; otherwise, it proves that he is not living in the spirit. If we lack inward peace while in tribulation, it proves that we are not living in the spirit; then if while having no tribulation we also have no inward peace, it is even more of a proof that we are not living in the spirit.

Therefore, concerning our condition in life, whether we are fleshly minded or spiritually minded, whether we are living in the flesh or living in the spirit, it is proved and made known to us through the sense of life. It is through this kind of proving that the sense of life gives us guidance from within. Only if we follow the guidance of this kind of proving can we live in life. Therefore, if we desire to go on in life, we must pay attention to the proving and leading which this sense of life gives us from within.

Chapter Six

THE FELLOWSHIP OF LIFE

In this book we are giving our attention to the matter of life, hoping to accomplish two things: first, to help every brother and sister know whether he or she has the experience of life we mention here or not; second, to lead brothers and sisters to understand the way of life thoroughly, so that later all may go to other places and speak it forth in spirit. This book is not for general teaching, but is a special investigation. We desire to bring forth all the things of life to see whether you have them. And if you do have them, can you speak them forth? Can you speak to touch others' feelings? Can you speak of them not only as doctrine, but also as experience? For this reason, we want not only to examine whether we have the things which every term of life denotes, but also to discover the definition and usage of every term.

There is a very heavy burden within me, a very deep feeling, that what every church today needs most is the things of life. All our work and activity must come out of life. This does not mean that we should not engage in much work and activity. It may be that our work and activity later will increase and be even more intensified than today. But unless it comes out of life, our work and service will neither last nor bear much weight. If we want our work to bear abundant and lasting fruit, we must have a foundation in life. We ourselves must touch the Lord in life and lead others to touch the Lord in life. Only thus can we fit into the work which God desires to do in this age.

All the results of our work should be measured by life. Only that which comes out of life is recognized by God. In Matthew 7, the Lord says that some preach the Gospel and some cast out demons, yet they are not approved by Him (vv. 22-23). Furthermore, the apostle in Philippians 1 says that some preach the Gospel out of envy (v. 15). Such works undoubtedly did not come out of life, but out of man's doings. We cannot and should not do such work. We should learn to live in the life of the Lord and allow His life to lead us to do His work. We should not aspire to some great work or to some accomplishment in work. We should have only one desire—to know and experience the life of the Lord more, and to be able to share with others what we have known and experienced so that they too may obtain something. When we work, we should not establish a work; neither should we set up an organization. Our work should just be the releasing of the life of the Lord, the imparting and supplying of the Lord's life to others. May the Lord have mercy upon us and open our eyes to see that the central work of God in this age is that man may gain His life and grow and mature in His life. Only the work which comes out of His life can reach His eternal standard and be accepted by Him.

In the last chapter we have seen the sense of life. Closely related to the sense of life is the fellowship of life. So let us now see the fellowship of life.

I. THE SOURCE OF THE FELLOWSHIP OF LIFE

Where does the fellowship of life come from? What is its cause? And from what is it derived? First John 1:2-3 says: "We [the apostles]...show unto you (the believers) the eternal *life*...that ye also may have *fellowship* with us: yea, and our *fellowship* is with the Father, and with his Son Jesus Christ." These verses show that the apostles preached unto us "the eternal life" so that we may have "fellowship." The eternal life is the life of God, and the life of God entering into us enables us to have fellowship. Since this fellowship comes out of the life of God, it is the fellowship of life. Therefore, the fellowship of life comes from the life of God; its existence is due to the life of God; it is derived from the life of God; and it is brought to us by the life of God. As soon as we obtain the life of God within us, this life of God enables us to have the fellowship of life. The life of God, therefore, is the source of the fellowship of life.

II. THE MEDIUM OF THE FELLOWSHIP OF LIFE

The life of God rests in the Holy Spirit of God, and it is through the Holy Spirit of God that the life of God enters into us and lives in us. Therefore, the fellowship brought to us by the life of God, though derived from the life of God, comes by means of the Holy Spirit of God. Hence, the Bible also calls this fellowship "the fellowship of the Holy Spirit" (2 Cor. 13:14, "communion" is "fellowship" in the original text).

It is the Holy Spirit who causes us to experience the life of God; therefore, it is the Holy Spirit who enables us to have fellowship in the life of God. All our fellowship of life is in the Holy Spirit and is caused by the Holy Spirit. That is why Philippians 2:1 says: "...any fellowship of the Spirit."

The Holy Spirit of God moves, requires, and urges within us to cause us to have the fellowship which comes from the life of God. Therefore, if we desire to have fellowship of life, we must not only have the life of God, but also live in the Holy Spirit of God. The life of God is the source of the fellowship of life, and the Holy Spirit of God is the medium of the fellowship of life. Although it is the life of God which gives us the fellowship of life, yet it is the Holy Spirit of God who causes us to practically enjoy this fellowship of life. Only when we are living in the Holy Spirit and walking by minding the Holy Spirit can we enjoy the fellowship of the life of God in a practical way.

III. THE MEANING OF THE FELLOWSHIP OF LIFE

Before we define the fellowship of life, one thing must be made clear. The life of God was originally in God, and later it entered into us who belong to God. Is this life of God which entered into us, then, a part or a whole? Our final judgment is that it is neither partial nor the whole, but that it is flowing.

Take for example the electricity in a light bulb. Is it the partial electricity, or is it the whole electricity from the power plant? The answer is that it is neither, because the same electricity which is in the power plant is also in these light bulbs. It is an electric current flowing continuously. Once the current stops, these light bulbs will cease to give light.

Take another example: the blood in my hand, is it local blood, or is it the blood of the whole body? If it were local blood, it then would have no communication; and if it were the blood of the whole body, it would also have no communication. But it is the circulating blood, the flowing blood. It is the blood of the whole body continuously circulating and unceasingly flowing. It is a whole as well as a part; and it is a part as well as whole.

So also is the life of God within us. It flowed out from God, and it flowed into thousands of saints, including us. This flowing life is from God; it passes through God, and it passes through thousands of saints, including us. Thus, it causes us to have fellowship with God and with thousands of saints.

It is just like a shining electric light bulb. The electricity in it is continuously flowing, thereby putting it in communication with the power plant and with many other shining light bulbs. This communication rests in the flowing of the electricity within it. Likewise, the fellowship of life in us also rests in the flowing of the life within us. The life of God within us brings a flow of life, and thus we have the fellowship of life. This fellowship of life enables us to be in touch with God and with thousands of saints as well. Therefore, the meaning of the fellowship of life is the *flowing* of life. This flowing of life is not separated from life; rather it is the fellowship of the flowing of life itself. This fellowship of the flowing of life requires that we continuously walk and live by following it and yielding to it. Whenever we do not follow it or yield to it, it stops flowing. Thus, the fellowship between us and God is severed, and the fellowship between us and the saints is also gone.

IV. THE FUNCTION OF THE FELLOWSHIP OF LIFE

What is the function or use of the fellowship of life? It is to inwardly supply us with all that is in the life of God or all that is in God. All the fullness in God is supplied to us through the fellowship of life. The more we allow the flowing of life to flow in us, the more we are inwardly supplied with the fullness of God. Such supply of the fellowship of life is like the circulating of the blood as the supply of the body and like the flowing of electricity as the supply of the lights.

The sense of life proves whether we are living in God or not. And the fellowship of life continuously supplies us with the things of life. Whenever your supply of life is cut off, it means that your fellowship of life is interrupted. If we continuously live in the fellowship of life, our supply of life will come continuously and unceasingly.

The fellowship of life and the sense of life are mutually related. As soon as the fellowship of life is interrupted, the sense of life causes us to feel we have lost the supply of life. When the fellowship of life is not interrupted, the sense of life causes us to feel that we have the supply of life. Therefore, whether we are living in the fellowship of life and whether we have the supply of life depends entirely on what the sense of life indicates. The more we live in the fellowship of life, the keener is our sense of life, and the more we are supplied with life.

Concerning the fellowship of life, it is sufficient to say this much. We should remember that the sense of life always tests and proves us, while the fellowship of life always supplies us. Our condition before the Lord is determined by the sense of life; and the supply of our spiritual life is received through the fellowship of life.

CHAPTER SEVEN

THE SENSE OF THE SPIRIT AND KNOWING THE SPIRIT

Now we shall see the seventh main point, namely, the sense of the spirit and knowing the spirit. Because every experience of life is in the spirit, knowing the spirit is a basic issue in the experience of life.

What really is this matter called the spirit? How can we know the spirit? How can we touch the spirit? I admit that such questions are not easy to answer. To explain what the spirit is like is rather difficult. To speak of the body is very easy, because we can see it and touch it. To speak of the soul is also not difficult, because, though the soul is abstract, we can feel it and know it by its functions and actions, such as thinking, considering, determining, decision-making, and being pleased, angry, sorrowful, and joyful. Only when we speak of the spirit is it truly difficult. Even understanding the spirit is not easy, not to mention speaking about the spirit. Nevertheless, we will still attempt to speak of it.

Romans 8 speaks of the spirit. It is difficult to find another place in the Bible which speaks of our condition in the spirit as clearly as this one. Therefore, if we want to know the spirit, it is imperative that we pay attention to this passage.

I. FOUR THINGS

In speaking of the spirit, the apostle uses four things:

A. Life

In verse 2 he says, "the Spirit of life." In so doing he shows us that the Spirit he speaks of here is the Spirit of life, the Spirit which is related to life, contains life, and belongs to life.

Then in verse 6 he says "to set the mind upon the spirit is life." This means that life is the fruit of the spirit, and the spirit is the origin of life; therefore, by touching the spirit we touch life. Life and the spirit are mutually related; hence, we can know the spirit through life. Although it may be difficult to know the spirit, yet it is relatively easy to apprehend life.

B. Law

In verse 2, the apostle speaks not only of "the Spirit of life," but even of "the law of the Spirit of life." This tells us that the Spirit he speaks of here not only belongs to life, but also has its law. Therefore, when he speaks of the Spirit, he speaks of life, and he speaks likewise of the law. He joins the three—life, Spirit, and law—together. Life and the Spirit cannot be separated; law and Spirit likewise cannot be divided. Life is the content and issue of the Spirit, whereas law is the function and action of the Spirit. By contacting life we touch the spirit; by sensing the law we also sense the spirit. Though the spirit is hard to find, the law is not difficult to seek. Therefore, by the law we can find the spirit.

C. Peace

In verse 6, the apostle says, "To set the mind on the spirit is life and peace." This means that the result of setting the mind on the spirit is not only life, but also peace. Therefore, life is the fruit of the Spirit, and peace is also fruit of the Spirit. When we touch the spirit, we touch life and we likewise touch peace. Just as life can make us apprehend the spirit, so also peace can cause us to realize the spirit.

D. Death

In verse 6, before the apostle says that setting the mind on the spirit is life and peace, he says, "To set the mind on the flesh is death." Here he uses something negative to bring forth by contrast the positive. Flesh and spirit are opposites, and so are death and life. Life is the fruit of the spirit and is derived from the Spirit. Death is the fruit of the flesh and is derived from the flesh. Life causes us to know the things derived from the spirit, thus enabling us to know the spirit from the positive side. Death causes us to know the matters derived from the flesh, thus unveiling the spirit from the negative side. Therefore, just as life enables us to know the spirit from the positive side, so death enables us to understand the spirit from the negative side. To know the spirit we need to know life, and we need to understand the opposite of life, which is death.

Thus, according to what the apostle says regarding these four things—life, law, peace, and death—they are closely related to the spirit both positively and negatively. If we thoroughly understand these four things, we can clearly know the spirit, which is very decidedly related to them. All these four things contain or convey a certain kind of consciousness.

II. CONSCIOUSNESS

Except for the lowest plant life, every life definitely has a certain consciousness. The higher the life, the richer is its consciousness. The life of the Spirit of life spoken of here is the life of God Himself, which is the highest life; therefore, it is the richest in consciousness. This life within us causes us to be full of spiritual consciousness, enabling us to sense the spirit and the things of the spirit.

Although the law of an unconscious object does not belong to the realm of consciousness, yet the law of a conscious life does belong to the realm of consciousness. For example, if I hit a brother, he immediately feels pain; if I stretch out my hand toward his eyes, his eyelids will immediately blink. He reacts in this way because in his body there is the law of life which compels him to do so. The moment I strike him, he feels pain—this is a law. The moment I stretch out my hand toward him, his eyes blink—this also is a law. Though these are laws, yet if you ask him what they are, he will say they are a matter of consciousness. This proves that the law of the physical life belongs to the order of consciousness. Since the life of the Spirit of life is the life of God, which is rich in consciousness, the law of the Spirit of life naturally is also full of consciousness.

The peace spoken of here is, of course, the peace within us.

The peace within is entirely a matter of consciousness. It is not likely that we could have peace within and yet not feel it. Therefore, the peace spoken of here is also a matter of consciousness.

Moreover, even the death spoken of here is a matter of consciousness. Death causes man to lose consciousness. When a man dies, he loses his consciousness. Therefore, when a man has no consciousness, it is proof that within him there is the working death; though he may not have died completely, he is nearly dead.

Furthermore, in spiritual matters, death not only causes us to lose the sense of life, it also causes us to have the sense of death. When we set our mind on the flesh, death becomes active in us. On one hand it causes us to lose the sense of life within, and on the other hand it causes us to have the sense of uneasiness, discomfort, depression, oppression, darkness, and emptiness. This kind of uneasy, uncomfortable, depressed, oppressed, dark, and empty feeling is the sense of death and causes us to sense death.

Thus, life, law, peace, and death—these four—all have a consciousness related to them. The consciousness of these things enables us to touch the sense of the spirit and thereby know the spirit. Therefore, we should spend some time to examine the consciousness of these four things.

III. THE SENSE OF LIFE

The life spoken of here refers to the life of the Spirit of life. Therefore, this life is of the Spirit, from the Spirit, and rests with the Spirit. The Spirit with which this life rests is not only the Spirit of God, but also our spirit. This Spirit is the Spirit of God *and* our spirit mingled as one spirit. In the Old Testament time, the Spirit of God only fell upon men, so that men received the power of God from without. He did not enter into man so that man could receive the life of God from within. Thus, in Old Testament times the Spirit of God was only the Spirit of power; it was not yet the Spirit of life. Not until the time of the New Testament did the Spirit of God enter into man as the Spirit of life so that man received the life of God from within. Today, in the New Testament time, the Spirit of God is not only the Spirit of power, but also the Spirit of life. He not only descends upon man, causing man to obtain the power of God outwardly, and He not only moves man, causing man to know his sin, confess, repent, and believe in the Lord; but He further enters into man, so that man may have the life of God inwardly, and He also dwells within man as the Spirit of life. When, upon being moved by Him we repent, believe, and receive the Lord Jesus as our Savior, He then enters into us and puts the life of God in us. At this time He enters into us as the Spirit of life, the Spirit of the life of God. The life of God is in Him, and He is thus the life of God; therefore, when He enters into us, the life of God enters into us. He enters into us with the life of God as the *Spirit* of life. When He enters, He enters into *our spirit,* not into our mind, emotion, or will. He enters into our *spirit,* puts the life of God in our *spirit,* and dwells in our *spirit;* thus, the Spirit of life is mingled together with our spirit. Now, the Spirit of God together with the life of God (He is the life of God itself) dwells in our spirit, so that He Himself, the life of God, and our spirit—all three—may mingle as one and never be separated.

We may use as an illustration a glass which originally has plain water within it. Later we blend into it some undiluted fruit juice with sugar added, so that it becomes a glass of water-sugar-juice, a three-in-one drink. The water signifies our spirit, the undiluted fruit juice represents the Spirit of God, and the sugar stands for the life of God. The Spirit of God containing the life of God mingles with our spirit, thus making these three—the Spirit of God, the life of God, and our spirit—a three-in-one spirit of life. This is what Romans 8:2 speaks of.

Thus, the spirit, in which rests the life of the Spirit of life which we are speaking of here, includes both the Spirit of God and our spirit. It is a spirit which is a mingling of the Spirit of God with our spirit. Bible translators have understood the Spirit mentioned in Romans 8 as the Holy Spirit; therefore, they have written Spirit with a capital *S*. Many readers of the Bible have also thought that the Spirit mentioned here refers only to the Holy Spirit. Yet spiritual fact and spiritual experience tell us that the Spirit mentioned here is the mingling of the Holy Spirit with our spirit. In verse 16 of this chapter, the apostle sets forth this spiritual fact (which is also our spiritual experience). He says: "The Spirit himself beareth witness with our spirit." By speaking in this manner, he clearly tells us that the spirit he mentioned before is the one spirit, which is the mingling of the "Holy Spirit with our spirit." To say that this spirit is the Holy Spirit is all right, and to say that it is our spirit is also not wrong. It is like the water in the glass with undiluted fruit juice. You may say that it is fruit juice, and you may also say it is water. This is because the two have become mingled as one. Likewise, the Holy Spirit and our spirit are also mingled as one spirit. Within this one spirit, which is the mingling of the two, there is the life which God bestows on us; thus, it becomes the spirit of life. Simply speaking, the life of God is in the Spirit of God, and the Spirit of God enters into our spirit; thus, the three are mingled as one and become the spirit of life.

Originally our spirit was merely the spirit of man, and it was dead. Now, when the Spirit of God enters, He not only quickens our spirit, but also adds the life of God into our spirit. Now not only is our spirit alive, but it also has the life of God; and it is not only a spirit; it is the spirit of life. All the consciousness of life in this spirit enables us to know this spirit. When we walk by setting our mind on this spirit, and when our actions and deeds are according to this spirit, the life in this spirit will cause us to have the consciousness of this life. Since this life is of God, fresh and lively, strong with power, bright and holy, real and not empty, the sense of this life surely will make us sense the presence of God; thus, we will feel fresh and lively, strong with power, bright and holy, real and not empty. When we have such feelings, we know we are minding the spirit, walking according to the spirit, and living in the spirit. Such feelings are the sense of life in our spirit, or the consciousness of our spirit of life, leading us from within to walk according to the spirit and live by the spirit. When we touch such feelings, we touch the spirit. When we heed such feelings, we heed the spirit. The spirit itself is relatively difficult for us to sense, but we can easily sense such feelings of life in the spirit. If we follow such feelings closely, we can then know the spirit and live in the spirit.

The life of God in our spirit can be said to be God Himself; therefore, the sense of this life surely will make us sense God Himself. If we live in the spirit and walk by minding the spirit, the sense of this life will cause us to feel that we are in touch with God, and that God is in us as our life, our power, and our all; thus, we will be happy, restful, comfortable, and satisfied. When we thus touch God in the inner sense of life, we touch life; thereby we know we are living in the spirit and setting our mind upon the spirit.

Since the spirit, in which rests the life of the spirit of life, is the mingling of God's Spirit with our spirit, then whatever this sense of life causes us to feel must be the story of the Spirit of God in our spirit. The Spirit of God in our spirit reveals Christ to us, imparts God in Christ to us, and causes us to experience Christ and contact God in the spirit. Thus, it causes us to experience Christ—that is, to experience God—as our life; this also means that it causes us to experience life, that is, to experience the life of God in our spirit. When we thus experience this life, it causes us to feel the satisfaction of life, the power of life, the brightness of life, the freshness of life, and the liveliness and transcendence of life. When we have such a sense of life within us, we know we are living in the spirit and touching the spirit.

IV. THE SENSE OF THE LAW OF THE SPIRIT OF LIFE

In the Spirit of life within us, there is not only the life of God, but also a law. This law is the law of the life of God. Every life has its law. The life in our body has its law within our body. That which agrees with its nature, its law approves and accepts; anything which is otherwise, its law opposes and refuses. Likewise, the life of God in our spirit also has its law. It is of the spirit and rests with the spirit; therefore, its nature is entirely and absolutely spiritual. If what we are and do agrees with its spiritual nature, this law in our spirit approves and accepts it; otherwise this law opposes and refuses. All that it approves and accepts is definitely from the spirit, because only that which is from the spirit can agree with its spiritual nature. Therefore, all that we are and do must be from the spirit and in the spirit; then the law of life in our spirit will approve and accept it.

This law of life in our spirit belongs to the order of consciousness and has its own consciousness. All that it approves and accepts or opposes and refuses is made known by what it feels and what it desires us to feel. If what we are and do is in the spirit and in agreement with the nature of the spirit of life in us, this law will make us feel that it approves and accepts it; otherwise, this law will cause us to feel that it is opposing and refusing. Thus, by the sense of this law, we can know whether or not we are living in the spirit and walking by the spirit. Since this law is the law of the spirit of life in us, the sense of this law is the sense of the spirit of life in us; therefore, the sense of this law can cause us to know the spirit within.

Law is a natural thing; therefore, the sense it gives us is also natural. For example, when we drink the glass of fruit juice, we naturally feel that it is sweet. This is because there is a law of the physical life in our body which naturally causes us to feel this. As soon as our lips touch the juice, we immediately taste the sweetness. This natural sense is the law of life of our body. This law naturally causes us to taste the flavor of the juice. The law of life in our spirit is also like this. We do not need others to tell us whether what we are and do as Christians is in the spirit, whether we are mindful of the spirit and pleasing to God; the law of life in our spirit will naturally make known our situation by giving us a certain sense. This natural feeling given to us by this law of life is a natural function of the spirit of life in us. By this we may easily discern whether or not we ourselves are living in the spirit.

Not only is the sense that this law of life gives us natural, but it also makes us natural. The more we live in the spirit and the more what we are and do agrees with the nature of the spirit of life within us, the more this law of life in our spirit will cause us to feel natural. If we as Christians are not natural, it proves we have some problem and that we are not living in the spirit. Since the spirit of life in us is a natural law of the spirit, only when our life and work agree with its spiritual nature can we feel natural within. When we feel natural within, it proves we are living in accordance with the law of life in our spirit. This natural feeling given to us by this law of life in us causes us to know we are living in the spirit and walking according to the spirit. Thus, if we follow the law of life in our spirit, or if we follow the natural consciousness given to us by this law of life, it means we are following the spirit of life within us. To put it simply, following the sense of the law of life in the spirit is following the spirit, because the sense of the law of life in the spirit is the sense of the spirit itself.

V. THE SENSE OF PEACE

The spirit of life in us is not only the place where the Spirit of God and the life of God dwell, it is also the place where the new man is. Furthermore, the spirit in us—the spirit mingled with the life of God—is also the new man within us. If in our outward action and behavior we mind the spirit of life within us, then we are living by the spiritual new man within us. In this way our inner man and outward actions are in agreement; hence, we feel natural and peaceful. We can say that this consciousness of being natural and peaceful is the result produced by the sense of the law of the spirit of life. If we mind the spirit of life within us, we naturally walk and live according to the law of the spirit of life within us. This causes us to feel natural from within and have the sense of peace. This sense of peace and the sense of life go hand in hand. The sense of life is fresh and lively; the sense of peace is natural and at ease. The sense of life is satisfaction and fullness of vigor; the sense of peace is rest and comfort. If we mind the spirit and walk and live by the spirit, we will not only have the sense of life, feeling fresh, lively, satisfied, and vigorous, but also have the sense of peace, feeling natural, restful, comfortable, and at ease. Such a sense is also the sense of the spirit. Once we have such a sense, we may know that we are living in the spirit. When we follow such a sense, we follow the sense of the spirit, which means that we follow the spirit. Such a sense enables us to know the spirit and recognize the spirit. The more we walk according to the spirit and live in the spirit, the richer and deeper this kind of sense within us becomes.

VI. THE SENSE OF DEATH

There is a contrast in Romans 8:6. The apostle says that the result of minding the flesh is death, whereas the result of minding the spirit is life and peace. This word reveals that just as the flesh is versus the spirit, so also the result of minding the flesh, which is death, is opposite to the results of minding the spirit, which are life and peace. Thus, the apostle tells us here that death is not only the opposite of life, but also the opposite of peace. Therefore, the sense of death is not only the opposite of the sense of life, but also the opposite of the sense of peace. The sense of life makes us feel fresh, lively, satisfied, and vigorous; the sense of death makes us feel the opposite of these—old, depressed, empty, and powerless. The sense of peace makes us feel natural, restful, comfortable, and at ease. The consciousness of death makes us feel just the opposite of these—unnatural, unrestful, uncomfortable, and uneasy. Thus, whenever we feel inwardly desolate, depressed, empty, dry, weak and powerless, dark and dull, or uneasy, insecure, uncomfortable, out of harmony, full of conflict, unnatural, sad, and bound, we should know we are not living in the spirit; rather we are living in the opposite of the spirit, which is the flesh.

The flesh the apostle speaks of here refers not only to the lusts of our flesh, but also to our entire old man. All that belongs to our inward new man belongs to the spirit; likewise, all that belongs to our outward old man belongs to the flesh. Whatever is not from the spirit and does not belong to the spirit is from the flesh and belongs to the flesh. Although the soul differs from the flesh, yet because the soul has already fallen and become captive to the flesh, all that is from the soul or belongs to the soul is also from the flesh and belongs to the flesh. Thus, if we live by the soul, we live by the flesh. Whether we are mindful of the flesh or mindful of the soul, we are nevertheless mindful of the flesh. The result of minding the flesh is death. This sense of death causes us to feel either depressed and empty or uneasy and insecure.

Whenever we have such consciousness, we should know that we are mindful of the flesh, and that we are living either in the flesh or in the soul. Such a sense causes us to know the opposite of the spirit, which is the flesh, and to recognize it. Thus, by knowing the opposite of the spirit, we may know the spirit itself.

Whatever we do, regardless of whether we think it is right or wrong, spiritual or unspiritual, if deep within us we feel restless, insecure, empty, and depressed, it proves that we are walking by the flesh and not living in the spirit. Even in prayer and preaching, not to mention other things or doing things which are not good, if we feel empty and depressed within, dissatisfied or unhappy, then it is proof that we are praying or preaching by the flesh, not in the spirit. Many times, by our mind or by the flesh (because it is not in the spirit), we pray as if we are reciting from a book. The more we pray, the more we feel dry and depressed, without watering and joy. After praying, we only feel empty; we do not feel satisfied. Such prayer by our head makes our spirit incapable of obtaining the supply of life; instead, it only touches the sense of death. Although what we prayed may have been quite appropriate, yet it was not in the spirit; therefore, we could not touch the watering and joy of life and peace, but sensed only the dryness and depression of death. Many times, our preaching is also like this. When we preach not according to the spirit but by our head, we feel empty and dry within, or we sense death; we do not feel satisfied or watered, and we do not have the sense of life. If we were in the spirit, if we spoke by the spirit, we should feel satisfied and restful within, which means we would sense life and peace. Thus, by such a sense, we can know whether what we do is in the flesh or in the spirit. Such a sense can cause us to know the flesh, and by knowing the flesh to know the spirit.

Death not only causes us to have such depressed, empty, uneasy, and unhappy feelings, but also makes us lose the sense of life. Such feelings of death are warnings to us, urging us to be delivered from the flesh and live in the spirit. If we have such a sense of death, yet we continue to act and behave by the life of the flesh, after a continued period of time, death can cause our spirit within to lose consciousness and become numb. If our spirit within is numb and unconscious, it is because we have lived by the flesh for such an extended period that our spirit is damaged by death. Thus, we can and we should know how we are treating our spirit and whether we are living in the spirit or not.

VII. KNOWING THE SPIRIT BY THE SENSE OF THE SPIRIT

All the senses of which we have spoken are those which the spirit of life within us causes us to have; therefore, we may say that they are the senses of the spirit. If we want to know the spirit directly, it is somewhat difficult, but it is comparatively easy to know the spirit itself by such senses of the spirit. We cannot quite apprehend directly what the spirit actually is, but by the sense of the spirit, it is not difficult for us to know it. If we walk and live by closely following the sense of the spirit, then we are following the spirit and minding the spirit. If we follow the naturalness of the law of the Spirit of life, take care of the sense of life and peace, heed the warning given to us by the sense of death, and live in these senses, then we are living in the spirit. These senses are from the spirit; therefore, they can cause us to touch the spirit and thereby know the spirit.

CHAPTER EIGHT

THE DIFFERENCE BETWEEN
SPIRIT AND SOUL

We have seen the sense of the spirit and knowing the spirit; now we shall see the difference between the spirit and the soul.

I. THE SEPARATION OF SPIRIT AND SOUL

The so-called psychologists analyze man and divide him into two parts: the metaphysical and the physical. The physical part refers to the body, and the metaphysical refers to the psyche, which is the soul spoken of in the Bible. They say that within the body of man there is only the psyche, the soul. But the Bible tells us that within man, besides the soul, there is the spirit. First Thessalonians 5:23 does not say only "soul" but "spirit and soul." The spirit and the soul are two things and are different. Thus, Hebrews 4:12 speaks of the dividing of soul and spirit.

If we desire to have true spiritual growth in life, we must know that the spirit and the soul are two different things, and we must be able to discern what is the spirit and what is the soul, what is spiritual and what is soulish. If we can discern the difference between the spirit and the soul, we then can deny the soul, be delivered from the soul, and live by the spirit before God.

A. Soul Versus Spirit

First Corinthians 2:14-15 speaks of two classes of man: one is the soulish man (the original text for "natural man" is "soulish man"), and the other is the spiritual man. This shows us that man can live by and belong to either of these two different things, the soul or the spirit. Man can either live by the soul and belong to the soul, thereby becoming a soulish man; or he can live by the spirit and belong to the spirit, thereby becoming a spiritual man. If a man is spiritual, he can then discern and receive the things of the Spirit of God; if, however, he is soulish, he cannot receive such things, and he cannot even know them. This makes it clear that the soul is in contrast to the spirit. The spirit can communicate with God and discern the things of the Spirit of God. To the soul the things of the Spirit of God are incongruous and inept. The spirit delights in appreciating and receiving the things of God, but the soul is not so; not only does it not receive such things, but it considers them foolish.

In the Bible, not only is there Romans 8, which shows us that the flesh is opposed to the spirit, but there is also 1 Corinthians 2, which shows us that the soul also is opposed to the spirit. When man lives by the flesh, he is of the flesh and not of the spirit; likewise, when man lives by the soul, he is of the soul and not of the spirit. Romans 8, when speaking of the flesh, emphasizes its relationship to sin; therefore, all who sin are fleshly. But the soul is not necessarily directly related to sin. Many times man may not sin and is not fleshly (as man sees it), yet still he is soulish and not spiritual. (Strictly speaking, when man is soulish, he is also fleshly, because the soul of man has fallen under the flesh. But when we speak of the soul itself, there is a difference between being of the soul and being of the flesh.) Thus, even if we do not sin and have been freed from sin, so that in man's eyes we are not fleshly, this does not mean that we are necessarily spiritual and not soulish; neither does it mean that we can surely understand the things of the Spirit of God, or that we can apprehend, appreciate, and receive the things of God. We often think that if we could only be freed from sin and cease from running wild in the flesh, we could then be spiritual, communicate with God, and understand the things of the Spirit of God. No, it is not so certain. It is quite possible that, though we seem to have been freed from sin and no longer run wild in the flesh, yet we still live by the soul and not by the spirit.

The salvation of the Lord delivers us not only from sin and the flesh, but also from the soul. The purpose of the Lord's salvation is not only that we should not be in sin and in the flesh, but also that we should not be in the soul, but in the spirit. His salvation would save us not only to the degree of morality that we become a moral man, but even more to the degree of spirituality so that we become a spiritual man. A man of good morals is not necessarily a spiritual man; on the contrary, it is quite possible that he is a soulish man, a man who lives by the soul. Thus, a brother or a sister may be very moral and very good; yet as to the spiritual things of God he or she may not be enlightened, may not desire or appreciate them, and even may not receive them, because he or she is living by the soul and is soulish.

B. The Impotence of the Soul
in Spiritual Things

First Corinthians 2:14 says: "the *soulish* man receiveth not the things of the Spirit of God...and he cannot know them." These words speak clearly and thoroughly concerning the condition of the soul as to the things of the Spirit of God. The soul "receiveth not" the things of the Spirit of God and "cannot know them." The soul does not desire the things of the Spirit of God, nor can it receive them; even if it wants to receive them, it cannot, because it cannot know or understand them. The nature of the soul is not in accord with the things of the Spirit of God; therefore, it neither wants nor receives the things of God. Moreover, it also has no ability to know the things of God. Therefore, as to the things of the Spirit of God, a man living by the soul has no feeling, no interest, and no desire; neither does he seek them, receive them, or even understand them. For this reason God must deliver us from the soul so that we do not live by the soul; then He can make us love, understand, and receive the things of His Spirit.

We must be clear concerning the impotence of the soul in spiritual things and regard it as an important matter. The soul does not receive the things of the Spirit of God and neither can it know them. A brother or sister who lives by the soul can be very good, well-behaved, and virtuous, but he

or she definitely cannot know spiritual things and may not
even thirst for spiritual things. I have met many such brothers and sisters. They are very careful in their conduct, and
their behavior may be said to be faultless, yet as to spiritual
things they have a mental block, and they do not seek them.
They evaluate themselves and others by the standard of
human morality, good and evil, right and wrong, and in all
matters they are short of the consciousness and insight of
the Spirit of God. It may be that they are clear in their mind
and strong in their intellect, but they are not enlightened
in their spirit, and the consciousness of their spirit is insensi-
tive. You may call them *good* Christians, but you cannot call
them *spiritual* Christians. As far as their conduct is concerned, they are really good. They know how to behave and
how to handle things; they are intelligent and alert, diligent
and thorough. But as soon as they touch the things of the
Spirit of God, they are lost. It is as if they were wood or stone,
with no consciousness or understanding faculty at all. Moreover, toward spiritual things they are often cold in heart; they
are not only slow in understanding, they are also slothful in
seeking.

Hence, good Christians are not necessarily spiritual
Christians. Spiritual Christians are not merely good in their
behavior; they live in the spirit, having the sense of the spirit,
understanding spiritual things, knowing the way of God from
within, and having proficiency in spiritual things. Goodness
and spirituality are very different. Many brothers and sisters
are good, but not spiritual; they are good, but they do not live
in the spirit. You meet goodness in them, but you do not meet
the spirit. You see the virtues of man in them, but you do not
smell the savor of God. From a certain standpoint, they do not
seem to be in the flesh, yet they definitely are in the soul.
Though they do not give rein to the flesh, they also do not live
in the spirit; though they do not approve of sinful things, they
also do not thirst after spiritual things; though they do not
sin according to the flesh, yet they live by self, which is the
soul. The soul is the source of their life, and it is also the
means of their living. They are soulish people, living in the

soul and by the soul; therefore they do not desire spiritual things, and neither can they understand them.

C. The Content of the Soul

The soul is our individual personality, our ego; therefore, the soul is our self. That which is included in the soul, analytically speaking, is the mind, the emotion, and the will—these three parts. The mind is the organ of man's thinking. It is what we usually speak of as the brain. (Physiologically it is the brain, and psychologically it is the mind.) It is the major part of the soul. Man's thinking, meditating, considering, and memorizing are all functions of the mind in the soul. Man after the fall, especially today's man, lives largely in the mind and is directed by the thoughts of the mind. As man thinks, so man behaves. Man's action is always tied to man's thought. There is hardly one who does not live in his thought. Thus, today, regardless of who or what we are considering, we must begin with man's thought in order to win man's mind. Nowadays, there are so many theories, schools, and educational methods, and they all have one aim: dealing with man's thought to win man's mind. If you can win a man's mind by his thought, you can then win him, because man lives in the mind, which is the brain, and is directed by the thought of the mind.

The emotion in the soul is the organ of man's love, anger, sorrow, and joy. Man loves, detests, rejoices, mourns, and is excited or depressed—these are all functions of the emotion in man's soul. There are many who are emotional. They are rich in emotion and very easily stirred. They often deal with matters by their emotion. With such people, when you reason with them in thought, it is often difficult to get through; but you can very easily move their emotion. They cannot be easily persuaded in the mind by you, but in the emotion they are easily moved.

The will in the soul is the organ of man's decision making. Man decides, determines, judges, chooses, receives, and refuses—these are all functions of the will in man's soul. Some people are in the mind, some are in the emotion, and there are some who are in the will. Just as those who are in the mind or emotion live in their mind or emotion, so those who are in the will likewise live in their will. As the mind or emotion respectively is the strongest part of those who are in them, so is the will. One who is in the will, is definitely very strong in his decision. Once he has determined upon some course of action, you have no way to change him. You may reason with him, but he does not care for reason; you may appeal to him with emotion, but he has no regard for emotion. He is one who acts by his will and is in the will.

That which is in the soul are these three parts—mind, emotion, and will. These three parts are simultaneously present in every man. Every man has thought, emotion, and will. However, some are more in the mind, some are rich in emotion, and others are strong in the will.

Some are very clear in their thinking. No matter how you try to move them with emotion, it is impossible. If you want to win them, you must use reason. They are living in the mind, or the brain; they are the intellectual ones.

Some especially abound in emotion. It seems as if they do not have a brain and do not think, but have only emotion. Such people often make a mess of things by their emotion. If you reason with them, they frequently neither care nor understand and are not moved in their heart. If you deal with them with emotion, it is very easy to touch their inward part. A thousand or ten thousand reasons are not as powerful toward them as one or two tears. Sometimes, no matter how you reason with them, you cannot convince them; yet if you only shed some tears, you can win them over. They only care for emotion, not for reason. This is because they are not in the intellect, but in the emotion.

Some people's will is especially strong. In everything they have some proposal or idea. And once they make a decision, they are very firm and cannot be easily changed. Such people usually are quite stable and stubborn, caring neither for emotion nor reason. In everything, by their obstinate will, they set forth ideas and establish policies. You reason with them, but they do not understand. You use emotion with them, but they are not moved. They are neither in the intellect nor in the emotion, but in the will.

II. THE SOULISH MAN AND THE SPIRITUAL MAN

A. The Soulish Man

Regardless of whether a man is in the mind, in the emotion, or in the will, he is soulish. Regardless of whether a man lives in the mind, in the emotion, or in the will, he lives in the soul. Regardless of whether a man lives by the mind, by the emotion, or by the will, he lives by the soul. Therefore, it is very easy for us to judge whether a man is soulish. We only need to see whether or not he acts by the mind, emotion, or will, and whether or not he lives in the mind, emotion, or will. As long as he acts and behaves by any one of these three, or as long as he lives in any one of these three, he is a soulish man.

A soulish man often is what man calls "a good man." He is frequently faultless in man's eyes. Clear thinking always brings the praise of man to those who act by it. Moderate emotion always brings the approval of man to those who live in it. A firm will also often brings the commendation of man to those who rely on it. But when man lives in these, though he is not living in sin, he is also not living in the spirit. Though before man he seems to be without sin and faultless, before God his spirit is blocked, and his spiritual understanding is dull.

Once in a certain place, I met a co-worker. His conduct was really good, but he lived too much in the mind, or the brain; therefore, it was difficult for him to understand or comprehend spiritual things. Whenever I spoke to him concerning matters of serving God, I was quite fearful that his eyeballs would turn. When I spoke, he would listen until he almost got the point, and then his eyeballs would turn, and he became confused again. When his eyeballs revolved, it meant that his mind was considering. He only used his mind to consider; he did not use his spirit to sense the things of God: therefore, it was exceedingly difficult for him to understand and sense spiritual things.

Thinking is frequently the difficulty and hindrance of the brothers in spiritual things. Many brothers often use thinking to deal with spiritual things. They think they can understand spiritual things by exercising their mind. They do

not know that the mind, being part of the soul, cannot understand the spirit. A man living in the mind lives in the soul
and definitely becomes a soulish man with no ability to
understand spiritual things.

Just as the mind is the difficulty of the brothers in spiritual things, so the emotion is frequently the hindrance of
the sisters. The reason many sisters cannot understand or
sense spiritual things is that they are too much in the emotion. In the churches of various places, I have seen many good
sisters who have enthusiasm and love, who are careful in
their behavior, and whose conduct is sober; yet when it comes
to spiritual things, they lack consciousness, and they can
hardly apprehend them. This is because they live too much in
their emotion and act too much by their emotion. Apparently,
emotion is not sin, but emotion prevents them from living in
the spirit, from touching the things of God by their spirit,
from having any spiritual sense, and from understanding
spiritual things. Emotion is their pitfall; it keeps them in the
sphere of the soul, living by the soul and being a soulish
person.

For many brothers, the will is also a difficulty and hindrance as to their understanding of spiritual things. Even
some sisters have this problem. They judge and decide on
matters too much by their will; so unknowingly they live
in the soul, having no spiritual sense or understanding in
spiritual things.

Whichever part of the soul a person is in, he will very
easily act by that part and live in that part. Whenever one
who is in the mind encounters anything, he will naturally
think through the matter again and again, considering it
from many angles. One who is in the emotion will uncon-
sciously care very much for the emotion in dealing with
others and handling things. One with a strong will very easily
leans on his will in dealing with man and matters, making
firm resolutions and unalterable decisions. Whichever part of
the soul a person lives in easily and naturally, he definitely
belongs to that part. If you see a person who very naturally
thinks, considers, weighs and measures every matter, you can
be sure he must be one who acts by the intellect; therefore, he

is one who is in the mind. If a person is easily stirred when facing things, smiling and weeping quickly, happy for one moment and depressed the next, you know that he must be one who abounds in emotion and is emotional. If whenever you encounter things, you plan and decide without any effort, and your will comes out to deal and function without any special exercise on your part, then undoubtedly you are one who is strong in will and who is in the will. Whichever part of the soul is strong or abounds in a person, it is always that part which is in the forefront whenever he encounters anything and deals with it. Whichever part of a person's soul takes the lead in dealing with things, it is a proof that he is in that particular part, and it is also a proof that he is a soulish man.

B. The Spiritual Man

If we can recognize what kind of person is soulish, it is not difficult to realize what kind of person is spiritual. Since a soulish person lives by the mind, emotion, or will, a spiritual person must be one who does not live by these. Since a soulish person lives by the soul and not by the spirit, then a spiritual person must live in the spirit and not in the soul. Although spiritual persons also have souls, and although the mind, emotion, or will in their soul may even be stronger and abound more than that of ordinary soulish persons, yet they do not live by these soulish organs, nor do they live in them. They live by the spirit and in the spirit, and they allow the spirit to be the master and source of all their action and behavior. The spirit in them occupies the preeminent position; it is the source of their behavior and starting point of their action. The soul in them is in the position of submission. Although the mind, emotion, and will in their souls also function, yet these are all subjected under the government of the spirit and are directed by the spirit. Although they use their mind, emotion, or will, yet they always follow the sense of the spirit in making use of these organs of the soul. They are not like soulish persons, who let the soul be the master in everything, who allow the mind, emotion, or will of the soul to stand in the forefront to lead and to function. They deny the preeminence of the soul and refuse the leading of the mind, emotion, or will. Thus, they allow the spirit to be the master in them; they allow the spirit to direct their whole being so that they may follow the sense of the spirit. Whenever they encounter something, they do not first use the mind, emotion, or will of the soul to contact and deal with it; rather, they use their spirit first to touch and to sense it, seeking first in the spirit for the Lord's feeling as to this matter. After they have touched the Lord's feeling in their spirit, they use the mind in the soul to understand the sense in the spirit, the emotion in the soul to express it, and the will in the soul to carry it out. Although they use the organs of the soul, yet they are not soulish, and they do not live by the life of the soul. They are spiritual, living by the life of the spirit, and the soul is but an organ for them to employ.

III. AN ABNORMAL CONDITION

We have seen that a fallen man, dead as he is in spirit, can only live by the soul. But we who are saved and have a quickened spirit can live by the spirit. Furthermore, God saves us so that we can return to the spirit and live by the spirit. The fall of man caused man to fall from the spirit to the soul, so that man no longer lives by the spirit but by the soul. God's salvation saves man from the soul to the spirit so that man does not live by the soul but by the spirit. However, many who are saved still do not live this way. Some remain in the soul and live by the soul because they do not know the difference between spirit and soul and the matters involved therein. Moreover, they do not know that God's desire is that they be delivered from the soul and live in the spirit. Although there are some who know that their spirit has been quickened, that it is different from their soul, and that God wants them to live in their spirit, yet they continue to remain in the soul and live by the soul. This is because they are accustomed to living by the soul and not by the spirit, and because they do not consider living in the spirit important. Those who do not know the difference between spirit and soul, and do not know God desires that we should be delivered from the soul and live in the spirit, think that to live by the mind, emotion, or will of the soul is fitting and necessary, and that if only they are

careful and faultless, they are all right. But they do not know
that as far as Christians are concerned, this is far too poor!

God does not intend to deliver us merely from faults to a
state of faultlessness; He intends to deliver us even more from
the soul to the spirit. He wants us not only to live a faultless
life, but even more to live a spiritual life, a spiritually faultless life. He wants us to live a faultless life not by the soul, but
by the spirit. Yet because of their ignorance, many Christians
still live by the soul, and they strive and struggle to be those
that are faultless by their soul life. Although their spirit is
already quickened, they do not know they should use their
spirit and live by their spirit. They want to make themselves
perfect men, living a satisfactory life by the power of the soul
alone. Their view and judgment of things and their love and
inclination are all in the soul, not in the spirit. Although they
are well-behaved Christians, and their conduct and behavior
are without fault, yet they still are living in the soul, not
in the spirit. Granted that their thoughts are clean, their
emotions are balanced, and their decisions are accurate, they
are still soulish, not spiritual. Their condition as far as
Christians are concerned is abnormal. They are living the
abnormal Christian life. Even if they can be successful, they
can only satisfy themselves. And sometimes some are really
satisfied with their success (a success which is really doubtful); but they cannot please God, for God wants man to be
delivered from the soul and live by the spirit.

Those who have some knowledge of the difference between
spirit and soul and of God's desire for us to be delivered from
the soul and live in the spirit, yet who are still living by the
soul, are also living an abnormal Christian life. Although
they know that their spirit is already quickened, yet they do
not live by it. Although they know that God wants them to be
delivered from the soul and live in the spirit, yet they still
remain in the soul and live by the soul. Although they know
that man should contact God in the spirit, yet they still use
the soul to touch the things of God. They know they have a
spirit, yet they do not use their spirit; they know they should
live by the spirit, yet they do not live in the spirit. They find
it convenient to use the mind, emotion, or will of the soul and

are not accustomed to using the spirit; hence, they neglect living by the spirit. Whenever anything happens, they always firstly use their mind, emotion, or will to deal with it. They do not firstly use their spirit to contact it. At most they can only be good and faultless Christians (and this is really doubtful); they cannot be spiritual Christians. They can only satisfy themselves; they cannot please God. They can only be commended by man; they cannot receive the praise of God. They still need the deliverance of God—not deliverance from sin, but deliverance from the soul; not deliverance from the filthy flesh condemned by man, but deliverance from the clean soul commended by man. Otherwise, they are still strangers and outsiders to the things of the Spirit of God.

IV. THE WAY OF DELIVERANCE FROM THE SOUL

How can we be delivered from the soul? This requires revelation from two standpoints: one concerning the soul, the other concerning the cross. We must see that the soul is impotent in the things of God and worthless in spiritual things. No matter how excellent and strong any part of our soul may be, it still cannot apprehend the things of God or understand spiritual things. However clean our mind, however balanced our emotion, and however proper our will, these can never make us spiritual. We must also see that our soul and all things that belong to it have already been crucified on the cross of Christ. In Galatians 2:20, when the apostle says, "I have been crucified with Christ," the "I" he refers to is the soul. The soul, in God's estimation, deserves only death. And our soul has already been taken care of by God through the cross of Christ. Hence, we should not value the things of our soul; rather we should only admit that our soul should die, that it deserves death, and that it is already dead. Such revelation and vision can enable us to condemn the soul, deny the soul, reject the soul, forbid the soul to take the lead in all things, and in everything give no ground to the soul. By the Holy Spirit we put the soul to death; we allow the Holy Spirit to put to death the soul life and to deal with the activity of the soul by the cross.

We must see how powerless the soul is before God, how

it cannot comprehend the things of God and cannot please God. We must also see God's estimate of the soul and how He deals with the soul. Only then can we deny the soul, reject the soul, and be delivered from the soul. Therefore, we must ask the Lord to make us see not only the impotence of the soul, but also the dealing of the cross with the soul; thus, in everything we will learn to reject the soul and not live by the soul. One who is in the mind should refuse his intellect in all spiritual things; he should put aside completely such functions as thinking and considering and return to the spirit, using the spirit to sense the consciousness of God. When he reads the Bible, prays or speaks about spiritual things, he should refuse his thinking, imagining, theorizing, and investigating, but follow closely the sense in his spirit and move on in the fellowship of God. One who abounds in emotion should refuse his emotion in everything; he should not allow his emotion to lead and direct, but let the Holy Spirit deal with his emotion; thus, he can sense the will of God in the spirit. He should fear his emotion just as he fears sin, and in fear and trembling live in the spirit, not being directed or influenced by his emotion. One who is in the will should see his will as the enemy of God in the things of God, as the opponent of the spirit. Thus, he will condemn, refuse, and deny his will. He should allow the Holy Spirit to break his will by the cross so that he will not live before God by his firm and strong will, but by the consciousness in his spirit.

Whichever part of the soul we are in, we should condemn and refuse it. Whether it is our mind, emotion, or will, they all should be broken and dealt with. In all things of God, we should refuse the leading of the mind, emotion, and will. Rather, we should let the spirit occupy the first place to govern, direct, and employ our mind, emotion, and will. In this way we can be delivered from the soul. Then on one hand we can employ all the organs in the soul by our spirit, and on the other hand we will not live by the soul; hence we will not be soulish but spiritual.

Chapter Nine

THREE LIVES AND FOUR LAWS

We now come to see the ninth main point in the knowledge of life—the three lives and four laws. This is a truth of extreme importance in the Bible. If we want to clearly know the condition of our inner spiritual life, or if we desire to lead an overcoming life free from sins, a thorough understanding of this basic truth is necessary.

I. THREE LIVES

A. The Definition of the Three Lives

The three lives spoken of here are the three lives that are within every saved one—man's life, Satan's life, and God's life.

Ordinarily, men think there is only one life within man, that is, the human life which is obtained from the parents. But the Bible shows that due to the fall of man, besides the human life, there is also in man the life of Satan. Therefore, Romans 7:18, 20 says that in man, that is, in the flesh of man, there dwells also Sin. Sin here refers to the life of Satan. This flesh, which contains the life of Satan, according to Galatians 5:17, continues to remain within man after he is saved, and often lusts against the Spirit. Therefore, after a person is saved, he still has Satan's life in him.

Moreover, John 3:36 says, "He that believeth on the Son hath eternal life." First John 5:12 also says, "He that hath the Son hath life," that is, the life of God. This shows that one who believes in the Son of God and is saved has not only his own original human life and the life of Satan obtained through the fall, but also the eternal life of God.

B. The Origin of the Three Lives

The Bible says that when God created Adam He breathed

into his nostrils the breath of life; thus, Adam obtained the created life of man. Then God put man in the Garden of Eden before two trees, the tree of life and the tree of the knowledge of good and evil. According to the revelations given later in the Bible, the tree of life signifies God, the tree of the knowledge of good and evil signifies Satan, and Adam represents mankind. Hence, that day in the Garden of Eden—that is, in the universe—a situation developed which involved three parties—man, God, and Satan.

Satan is the opponent of God, and the focus of his struggling with God is man. Both Satan and God wanted man. God desired man for the accomplishment of His will, while Satan wanted man for the fulfillment of his evil desire. The method of both Satan and God in gaining man was through life. God's intention was for man to eat the fruit of the tree of life and thus obtain His uncreated life and be united with Him. However, Satan enticed man to eat the fruit of the tree of knowledge of good and evil, thus causing man to obtain his fallen life and be mixed with him.

On that day, Adam, deceived as he was by Satan, ate of the fruit of the tree of the knowledge of good and evil. Henceforth, Satan's life entered into man, causing him to become corrupted. Thus, besides his own original created life, man also obtained the fallen life of Satan.

In the New Testament time, God put His life in His Son to be manifested among men, so that by believing in His Son and receiving Him, man may obtain His life. Thus, besides our original created human life and the life of Satan obtained through the fall, we also obtain the life of God.

Therefore, the three lives within us who are saved are obtained through creation, the fall, and salvation, respectively. Coming forth from the creating hands of God, we obtained the created human life. Passing through Adam, we became fallen and obtained the fallen life of Satan. Getting into Christ, we are saved and obtain the uncreated life of God.

C. The Location of the Three Lives

According to scriptural revelations, the three different lives of man, Satan, and God entered respectively into our soul, body, and human spirit—the three parts of our being. When God formed man of the dust of the ground, He breathed into him the breath of life, and "man became a living soul" (Gen. 2:7). This means that the human life obtained through creation is in man's soul. When man was enticed by Satan and fell, he ingested into his body the fruit of the tree of knowledge of good and evil, which signifies Satan. Therefore, the life of Satan obtained by man through the fall is in the human body. When man receives the Lord Jesus as Savior and is saved, the Spirit of God, bringing with Him the life of God, enters into the human spirit. Hence, the life of God obtained by man through salvation is in the human spirit. Thus, a person who is saved has the life of God in his spirit, the human life in his soul, and the life of Satan in his body.

In order to understand more clearly the three parts wherein the three lives are located, we shall spend a little time to discuss the consciousness of these three parts. The body, our outermost, physical part, is visible and touchable; it includes all the members of our body and has the five senses of seeing, hearing, smelling, tasting, and touching to contact the physical world. Therefore, the consciousness of the body is called the worldly sense or physical sense.

The spirit, our innermost and deepest part, includes the conscience, intuition, and fellowship. The conscience is the organ for distinguishing right and wrong; and, according to the principle of right and wrong, it causes us to sense what is right and accepted in the eyes of God and what is wrong and rejected in the eyes of God. The intuition enables us to sense the will of God directly, without the need of anything as a means. The fellowship part enables us to communicate and fellowship with God. Although it is the fellowship part that causes us to contact God, yet it is both the conscience and the intuition that cause us to sense God and spiritual matters, that is, to contact the spiritual world. The sense of these two parts is the sense in the spirit; hence it is called the spiritual sense, or the sense of God.

The soul, which is situated between the spirit and the body, is our inner, psychological part and includes the mind, emotion, and will. The mind is the organ for thinking and considering; the emotion is the organ for pleasure, anger, sorrow, and joy; and the will is the organ for formulating opinion and making decisions. Although the soul consists of three parts, only two—the mind and emotion—have consciousness. The sense of the mind is based on rationalization, whereas the sense of the emotion is based on likes and dislikes. The two senses in our soul enable us to sense man's psychological part, that is, man's ego or self, and to contact the psychological world; hence, they are called psychological senses or self-consciousness.*

D. The Nature and Condition of the Three Lives

Since each of the three different lives which we obtained within us has its own origin and dwells separately in one of the three different parts of our being, then the nature of these three lives and their respective conditions within us must also be different and rather complicated. Immediately after man was created in the hands of God, in God's eyes he was "very good" (Gen. 1:31) and "upright" (Eccl. 7:29). Therefore, the created life of man was originally good and upright; not only was it without sin, but also without the knowledge of sin and the consciousness of shame; it was innocent and simple.‡

After Adam sinned and fell, man not only offended God in behavior, which resulted in a sinful situation, but, worse still, he was poisoned by Satan in life, which caused his life to become defiled and corrupted. For example, suppose I instruct my children at home not to play with a blackboard

* Ordinarily when we say "man's consciousness," we refer to the sense of likes and dislikes in the emotion of the soul. Although this sense can be affected by the mind of the soul, the five senses of the body, and the conscience of the spirit, or even slightly affected by the intuition of the spirit, as in the case of a spiritual man, yet it is mainly constituted of the sense of likes and dislikes in the emotion of the soul.

‡ After the fall, God caused man to have the sense of shame. This sense has a twofold function: on one hand it proves that we have sin, and on the other hand it hinders us from committing sin. If a person does not have a sense of shame, he is apt to commit sin at will. The more sense of shame anyone has, the more he will be kept from committing sins. We have a saying that women ought not to be shameless. One who is void of the sense of shame is surely a person of the lowest class.

eraser. After I leave home, due to their curiosity, they play with the eraser; and then upon my return, I find that they have done wrong. This wrongdoing is merely a violation of the family regulation; nothing has gotten into them. Suppose, however, that next time I leave a bottle of poisonous medicine at home and tell the children, "Don't ever drink this." After I leave home, they find that the bottle is fun to play with—and, alas, they drink the poisonous medicine. At this point, they have not only disobeyed my order and violated the family regulation, but, worse still, something poisonous has gotten into them. This is what happened when Adam ate the fruit of the tree of knowledge that day. Not only had he disobeyed God's prohibition, but he also had taken Satan's life into himself. Henceforth, man became inwardly complicated; he not only had the original upright and good life of man, but also the evil and corrupted life of Satan.

Satan's life, filled as it is with all kinds of sins, contains the seed of all corruption and factors of evil. Satan lives within man and causes him to have lusts (John 8:44) and commit sins (1 John 3:8). Therefore, his life is the root of sins, which causes man to live out sin. The various sins committed by man are derived from the life of Satan or the life of the devil within him. Ever since this devilish life entered into man, though at times he is still able to live out a little human goodness according to his human life, he lives out the devilish evils most of the time according to the devilish life. Sometimes man can be very gentle; he can really act like a man and give forth the savor of a true man. But other times, when he loses his temper, he is really like a devil and full of the devilish odor. When man indulges in drunkenness and carousing, visiting prostitutes, gambling, and committing various sins, he bears a devilish appearance and is full of devilish odor. It is not of his own will that man lives out the devilish life; rather it is the life of the devil within that tricks him and thus causes him to become a devilish man and lead the life of a mixture of man and devil.

This is the actual inner condition of the people of the world today. Due to the fact that man has the lives both of man and of Satan, one good in nature and the other evil, he has the desire on one hand to be good and upright, and on the other hand he has an inclination toward corruption and evil. Hence, throughout the generations, philosophers engaged in the studies of human nature have advocated two different thoughts: one, that man is good in nature, and the other, that the nature of man is evil. Actually, we have both these natures within us, because we have within us both the life of good and the life of evil.

But, thank the Lord, today we who are saved not only have the lives of man and the devil, but also the life of God. Just as Satan, through his corruption, injected his life into us and caused us to be united with him, gained by him, and possessed of all the evils of his nature; so also God, through His deliverance, puts His life into us and causes us to be united with Him, gained by Him, and possessed of all the divine goodness of His nature. Therefore, just as the crucial point of the fall was life, so also the crucial point of salvation is life. When we come to the Lord's table, we break the bread of life first, and then we drink the cup of remission. This signifies that when we experience the Lord's salvation, although first we receive the blood and then the life, yet in His salvation the main figure is the bread, which signifies life. The cup, which signifies the blood, is secondary. Hence, first we take the bread, and then the cup.

When the life of God enters into us, we become more complicated within than the worldly people. We have the upright life of man, the evil life of Satan, and the divinely good life of God. This means that we have man, Satan, and God. The tripartite situation of man, God, and Satan which existed on that day in the Garden of Eden exists also in us today. We can say that inside of us is a miniature Garden of Eden with man, God, and Satan—all three—there. Therefore, Satan's struggle with God for man in the Garden of Eden is also occurring in us today. Satan moves within us today, desiring that we cooperate with him so that he can fulfill his evil intention of possessing us; God also moves within us, desiring that we cooperate with Him to accomplish His good pleasure. If we live according to the life of Satan within us, we will live out the evils of Satan and thus enable him to fulfill his evil intention upon us. If we live according to the life of God within us, we will live out the divine goodness of God and thus enable Him to accomplish His good pleasure in us. Although sometimes it seems that we can be independent and live neither according to the life of Satan nor according to the life of God, but only according to our human life, yet actually we cannot be independent; either we live according to the life of God, or we live according to the life of Satan.

Consequently, a Christian can act as three different kinds of persons and live three different kinds of lives. A brother who is very affable in the morning really looks like a man; at noon, when he gets angry with his wife, he resembles a demon; and at night, when in his prayer time he feels that he has wronged his wife and confesses both before God and to his wife, he appears like God. Thus, within one day he acts like three different persons, living out three different conditions. In the morning he is affable as a man, at noon he loses his temper as a demon, and at night, after dealing with sin, he manifests the likeness of God. Within one day, man, the devil, and God are all manifested in his living. The reason he can act in such a way is that within him there are the lives of all three—man, the devil, and God. When he lives according to the life of man, he is like a man; when he walks according to the devilish life, he is like the devil; and when he acts according to the life of God, he manifests the likeness of God. Whichever life we live in accordance with, regardless of the life, that life determines what we will live out.

Hence, we must see clearly that within a person who is saved there are three different lives—the created life of man, the fallen life of Satan, and the uncreated life of God. Though we have all three lives within us, yet we obtain them at three different junctures due to three different occurrences. First, at the time of creation and through creation we obtained the created life of man. Second, during the fall, due to our contact with Satan and the tree of knowledge of good and evil, we obtained the fallen life of Satan. Third, at the time of our salvation, because we believed in the Son of God and received Him, we obtained the uncreated life of God. Due to the fact that these three events—creation, fall,

and salvation—occurred in us, we obtained the three lives of
man, Satan, and God, each life differing from the others in
nature. Having seen and known this, we can then be clear
regarding the way of life. Since the three different lives of
man, Satan, and God exist in us concurrently, according to
which one should we live? The life of man? The life of God? Or
the life of Satan? The life we live in accordance with is the life
we will live out. Herein lies the way of life.

II. FOUR LAWS

Each of the three lives within us who are saved has a law.
Therefore, there are not only three lives within us, but also
three laws which belong to the three lives. Besides these,
there is the law of God outside of us. Therefore, within and
without us, there are all together four laws. This is revealed
to us in Romans 7 and 8.

A. The Definition of the Four Laws

The central theme of Romans chapters seven and eight is
law. Earlier, in chapter six, the apostle says, "For sin shall not
have dominion over you: for ye are not under law." The only
reason sin cannot have dominion over us is that we are not
under the law. Therefore, in order to explain the statement
that we are "not under law," the apostle continues to speak
about law in chapters seven and eight. Chapter seven begins
by saying, "Or are ye ignorant, brethren (for I speak to men
who know the law), that the law hath dominion over a man
for so long time as he liveth?" Again, "But now we have been
discharged from the law, having died to that wherein we were
held" (v. 6). Later he says, "I had not known sin, except
through the law" (v. 7). Again, "For I delight in the law of God
after the inward man" (v. 22). All these refer to the law of
the Old Testament. Finally, he says, "But I see a different
law in my members, warring against the law of my mind,
and bringing me into captivity under the law of sin which is
in my members." And again, "So then I of myself with the
mind, indeed, serve the law of God; but with the flesh the law
of sin" (v. 25). Then in chapter eight he says, "For the law of
the Spirit of life in Christ Jesus made me free from the law

of sin and of death" (v. 2). In these words the apostle speaks all together about four different laws that are related to us personally.

First is "the law of God" (7:22, 25), that is, the law of the Old Testament, which tells forth all God's requirements upon us. Second, "the law of the mind" (7:23), which is in our mind, causes us to desire to do good; therefore, it may also be called the law of good in our mind. Third, "the law of sin in the members" (7:23) causes us to sin. Because the function of this law in us which causes us to sin is manifested in the members of our body, it is called "the law of sin in the members." Fourth, "the law of the Spirit of life" (8:2) causes us to live in the life of God. The Spirit from which this law is derived is the Spirit of life, a mingled spirit composed of the Spirit of God, the life of God, and our human spirit. Therefore, it is called "the law of the Spirit of life." Furthermore, since this Spirit contains life, belongs to life, and is life, the law of this Spirit is called "the law of life." Concerning the four laws, one is outside of us—the law of God; while the other three are inside of us—the law of good in the mind, the law of sin in the body, and the law of the Spirit of life in our spirit.

B. The Origin of the Four Laws

The origin of each of the four laws differs. The law of God, written on stone tablets, was given by God to men through Moses during Old Testament times. The other three laws are derived from the three lives which we mentioned earlier. We know that with every life there is a law. Although a law may not always be derived from a life, nevertheless a life always has a law. Since we have three different lives within us, we have three laws corresponding to the three different lives.

The law of good in the mind is derived from the good created life, which was obtained not at the time of our salvation but at the time of birth. It is a natural endowment in God's creation, not a gift in God's salvation. Before we were saved, there was frequently in our mind and thought a natural inclination or desire to do good, to honor our parents, to be benevolent to men, or to be remorseful, hoping to reform ourselves and determining to go upwards. These thoughts of doing good and going upwards are derived from the law of good in our mind. They also prove that, even before we were saved, this law of good was already within us.

Some people, based on Romans 7:18 ("For I know that in me...dwelleth no good thing") conclude that either before we were saved or after we are saved there is no good thing within us; therefore, the law of good which is in our mind cannot be derived from our original created life, much less exist before we were saved. However, if we read Romans 7:18 carefully, we see that this conclusion is inaccurate, for when Paul says that there is no good thing within us, he is referring to the condition in our flesh. And the flesh spoken of here, according to the context of verses 21, 23, and 24, refers to our fallen and transmuted body. In our fallen and transmuted body, that is, in our flesh, there dwells no good thing. This does not mean that there is no good thing at all in us fallen beings. On the contrary we are told clearly later in the chapter that within us fallen beings there is a will which desires to do good and a law of good in our mind. Both the will and the mind are parts of our soul. Therefore, although there is no good thing in our fallen and transmuted body, there is an element of goodness in both the mind and will of our soul, even after the fall. This element of goodness naturally belongs to our good created life. Therefore, the law of good in our mind is of our original created life and existed before we were saved, even at our birth.

Some may say that our good created life, having been corrupted by Satan through the fall, has lost its element of goodness. This is also inaccurate. For example, adding a sour element into a glass of honey-water damages the sweet taste, but does not eliminate the sweet element. Although man has been damaged by Satan, his element of goodness still remains. It is a fact that the element of goodness created in man has been corrupted by Satan and has thus become incurable, but we cannot say that it has been corrupted to the point of non-existence. If you smash a glass, it will disintegrate into pieces, but its element still remains. A piece of gold bar may be thrown into a filthy pool, but the element of gold still exists. Although our honor to parents, brotherly love, loyalty, sincerity, propriety, morality, modesty, and sense of shame are rather impure and mixed, yet these elements are genuine. Therefore, we can conclude that although our good elements have been defiled, they still remain after the destruction; though they are very weak, still they remain. It is for this reason that the Chinese sages and philosophers have discovered that within man there are some "illustrious virtues," and "innate consciousness," etc., and have concluded that the nature of man is good. The discovery of these philosophers concerning human nature is indeed right, because within us fallen beings there is still the element of goodness and the law which naturally causes us to desire to do good.

The law of sin in the members is derived from the fallen and evil life of Satan. We have said before that due to Adam's fall through sinning—eating the fruit of the tree of knowledge of good and evil—Satan's life entered into man. Within this life of Satan there is contained a law of evil, that is, the law of sin in the members. Since the life of Satan is evil, the law which is derived from his life naturally causes man to sin and do evil.

The law of the Spirit of life is derived from the Spirit of life which is in our spirit and from the uncreated divine life of God. When we received the Lord and were saved, the Spirit of God together with the life of God entered into our spirit and mingled with our spirit to become the Spirit of life. In this life of the Spirit of life, there is contained a law which is the law of the Spirit of life, or the law of life.

Therefore, we must see clearly that when we were saved, God did not put the law of good in us; rather He put the law of life in us. God's purpose in us is life, not goodness. When God saves us, He puts the law of life in us. The law of good is not given through God's salvation, but through His creation. The element of doing good that is in us is inherent. But when God saves us, He puts His life in us. In this life there is contained a law of life, the law of the Spirit of life. This law is obtained at the time of our salvation and is derived from God's salvation of life.

Therefore, concerning the origin of these four laws we can say that the law of God, derived from God, is of God; the law of good in the mind, derived from the life of man, is of man; the law of sin in the members, derived from Satan's life, is of Satan; and the law of the Spirit of life, derived from the Spirit of life, is of the spirit.

C. The Location of the Four Laws

In order to have a precise knowledge of the four laws, we must be clear about their respective locations.

The law of God is written on tablets of stone; hence, it is outside of us.

The law of good is in our mind, that is, in our soul. Since the life of doing good is in our soul, the law which is derived from this life is also, of course, in our soul. The function of this law is especially manifested in the mind of our soul; hence this law is called "of the mind." Therefore, in our soul we have the life of man, the law of good which is derived from such a life, and the good human nature.

The law of sin is in our members, that is, in our body. During man's fall, he took the fruit of the tree of knowledge into his body; hence, the evil life of Satan entered into our human body. Thus, the law of sin, derived from the life of Satan, is also in our body. Since this law is in our body and the body is composed of the members, this law is in our members. Thus, in our body we have Satan, the life of Satan, the law of sin which is derived from the life of Satan, and the evil nature of Satan. Due to the fact that Satan and his evil things entered into our body and mixed with it, it was transmuted and became the corrupted flesh.

The law of the Spirit of life is in our spirit. Since the Spirit of life together with the life of God dwells in our spirit, the law derived from the Spirit of life is also in our spirit. This law is derived from the Spirit of God and is in our spirit; therefore, not only is its origin Spirit, but its location is spirit. Hence it is entirely of the spirit; it is neither of the body nor of the soul. Thus, in our spirit we have God, the life of God, the law derived from the Spirit of God's life, and His nature of life.

D. The Nature and Function of the Four Laws

What are the nature and functions of these four laws

outside and inside of us? The law of God is composed of the statutes of God, and its nature is holy, righteous, and good. This law, being outside of us, enables us to know what God condemns and what He justifies; it requires us to reject what God condemns and do what God justifies in order to comply with God's holy, righteous, and good statutes.

The law of good in our mind, derived from our created, human life of good, contains the good human nature and exactly fits the nature of the law of God outside of us. This law creates in us, that is, in our mind, the desire to do good. Especially when the law of God outside of us requires us to be good, this law of good in us gives us the inclination toward doing good. Therefore, the mind in us delights in obeying the law of God outside of us. This is what the apostle says, "I of myself with the mind, indeed, serve the law of God" (Rom. 7:25).

The law of sin in our members, derived from the evil and fallen life of Satan in our flesh, contains the evil nature of Satan. The evil life of Satan is the "evil" that is present in our flesh and the "sin" that dwells within us (Rom. 7:21, 20). The law that comes out of this evil life causes us to sin, because it is a "law of sin." This law displays from our flesh its natural power to do evil and wars against the law of good in our mind. When the law of good in our mind gives us the desire to do good, this law of sin rises to war against it and brings us into captivity (Rom. 7:23). Hence, not only are we unable to fulfill our desire to do good or to satisfy the good requirement of God's law; on the contrary, we obey the law of sin in our members, committing all kinds of sins and obtaining death, just as described in Romans 7:21-24. Therefore, we sin not of our own choice nor of our own volition; rather it is the law of sin which motivates us from within.

Hence, we can see here that within us fallen beings there are two contradicting laws. One is derived from the created life of good and works in the mind of our soul, giving us the desire to do good. The other is derived from the fallen, evil life of Satan and works in the members of our body, causing us to commit sin. These two opposite laws, doing contradictory works in our mind and in our members, war against one another within us. The result is that the law of sin usually overcomes the law of good; hence we fail to do the good which we desire and are forced to do the evil which we do not want to do. This is what the Chinese call the war between reason and lust. Reason is the element of doing good, inherent in our created life; lust is the sin that dwells in our fallen body, or the evil that is in our flesh. Although reason is partly derived from our human conscience, it works in our mind; hence the goodness resulting from the outworking of "reason" is either derived from or passes through the intellect. Although lust is related to our fallen human nature, it works in the members of our body; hence the evil which is the outworking of lust is derived from the lust. For this reason, one who is strong in intellect is more capable of doing good, while one who is more passionate easily does evil. In other words, all the good done by men either originates from or passes through the intellect in the mind, whereas all the evil done by men is the outworking of the lusts in the members. When the reason in our mind gains the position of advantage, it causes man to do good; when the lust in the members gains the superior position, it causes man to do evil.

Some people think that this kind of war is the same as the strife mentioned in Galatians 5. This is not accurate. Galatians 5 speaks about our flesh striving against the Spirit; this occurs only after we are saved and have obtained the Holy Spirit. But the war between the two laws is related to the war between the fallen, evil life of Satan and the created life of good, and this war exists even before we are saved. Therefore, this is an inner war existing before we are saved. It is also a war between good and evil existing in all worldly people.

This "Sin," out from which came the law of sin, is the life of Satan and is therefore alive. "Sin," shown capitalized, signifies that it is personified and is unique. In the universe there is only one God, and there is only one Sin. Sin is a special term and a unique object; Sin is another name of Satan. Therefore, Romans 5 to 8 tells us that Sin can reign over us, have dominion over us, cause us to be his slave in opposition to God, dwell in us, and overpower us, causing us to do the evil which we would not. The many sins outside of us are but the actions resulting from the working of the unique Sin within us. This unique Sin is the root and mother of all sins.

How does Sin cause us to sin outwardly? We have seen that Sin dwells in our body. However, it is the will, not the body, that is the motivating organ. The will, which belongs to the human soul, being controlled by Sin and obeying the orders of Sin, instigates the human body to commit sin. Hence, although Sin dwells in our body, its damaging work advances from the circumference to the center. With the body as the base, it projects forth the poison of sin, causing damage to our soul and spirit, until our whole being is corrupted. Therefore, Jeremiah 17 says, "The heart is deceitful above all things." Romans 1 and Mark 7 also declare that there are all kinds of sins within man. These scriptures prove that man is completely corrupted by Sin within and is full of sins. Hence, in the soul of man today, his mind is evil, his emotion defiled, his will rebellious, and even his spirit darkened. These are the results of the work of Sin in man.

But we must thank the Lord, for in us who are saved there are not only the two laws of good and of evil, of man and of Satan; there is also the law of the Spirit of God's life. Since this law is derived from the Spirit of God's life, it comes from the uncreated, divine life of God. As far as the nature of being both divine and eternal is concerned, of all the so-called lives in the universe, only the life of God is "life." (This has been discussed in detail in chapter one, *What Is Life?*) Therefore, the nature of God's life is "life." Since the law of the Spirit of life is derived from the life of God, its nature is "life," just as the nature of the life of God is "life." It is not like the two previously mentioned laws which are either "good" or "evil" because of the life from which they are derived.

According to scriptural revelation, life and good are different. Here we have three main points: first, life is the nature of the life of God, whereas good is the nature of the life of man; second, life is good, but good is not necessarily life; third, the tree of life and the tree of good and evil in the Garden of Eden show us that life and good are definitely different; life is neither good nor evil. Life, good, and evil are three different and independent things.

We should realize not only that life and good are not the same, but that good differs from good. There is the good of God, and there is also the good of man. God's good comes from the life of God and contains the nature of God's life. Man's good comes from the life of man and contains only man's good nature. The good mentioned in Ephesians 2:10 and 2 Timothy 2:21 is the good which we live out through the life of God; hence it is the good derived from the life of God and is God's good. The good mentioned in Matthew 12:35, Romans 7:18, 19, 21 and 9:11 is the good which we live out according to our own life; hence it is the good derived from the life of man and is the good of man. The good derived from the life of man is but the good of man, without the nature of "life" or the element of God. Only the good of God derived from the life of God is not only good, but also possesses the nature of "life" and God's very element. Therefore, when we say that life and good are different, we mean that the life *of God* and the good *of man* are different. The good of man, derived from the life of man and containing nothing of the life nature of God, naturally differs from the life of God. However, since God's good is derived from the life of God and contains the life nature of God, we cannot say that it differs from the life of God.

Thus, we see that the law of the Spirit of life containing the "life" nature of God can cause us to live out the life of God, that is, to live out the good of God.

Moreover, these three different laws within us differ also in their degree of strength. We know that laws vary in strength according to the degree of strength of the objects of their respective origins. The law of good is derived from the life of man, and the life of man is the weakest; hence the strength to do good of the law of good is also the weakest. The law of sin is derived from the stronger life of Satan; hence this law's power of sinning is stronger than the power of doing good of the law of good; it not only disables us from doing good, but it causes us to commit sin and do evil. The law of the Spirit of life is derived from the strongest life, the life of God; hence the power of this law is also the strongest; it not only keeps us from obeying the law of sin to commit sin, but

also enables us to obey itself and live out the life of God naturally.

Philosophers throughout generations have advocated various ways of cultivating morality or improving behavior. In
fact, what they have advocated is a working through human
intellect, self-will, and self-effort on the already corrupted
body and soul, in order to restore or reactivate the original
good in man. All this cannot overcome the natural power of
the law of sin. The strength of man is limited, while the power
of the law is enduring; man's striving is a self-exertion, while
the power of law is spontaneous. Man by using his own effort
may be able to sustain himself for a while, but once his
strength is exhausted, the power of law manifests itself
again. Therefore, God's way of deliverance is not to work on
our outward body by dealing with the Sin which surrounds
us, nor to work on the soul, which is between our body and
our spirit, by strengthening our will to do good. But it is in
our center, that is, in our spirit, that God adds into us a new
element, which brings with it a mighty power of life. Then He
advances from our center to the circumference, penetrating
through all the parts of our being, by using one law to subdue
another law to overcome the power of sinning in the law of
sin. Moreover, we are enabled to live out the good required by
the law of God, which we were unable to live out formerly
through the law of good. And much more, through the life
which is derived from the law of the Spirit of life, we are able
to live out the life which God desires.

Therefore, the Bible shows us that there are four laws
related to us, one outside of us and three inside us. The one
outside us is the law of God. Of the three that are inside us,
one is in our soul, one in our body, and one in our spirit. The
law in our soul, derived from the created, good human life,
is good and gives us the desire to do good; the law in our body,
derived from the fallen, evil life of Satan, is evil and causes us
to sin; the law in our spirit, derived from the uncreated,
divine life of God, is divine and causes us to live out the divine
life of God.

The law of God outside of us represents God in giving
us the requirements of holiness, righteousness, and goodness.

The law of good in our soul, upon touching the holy and good
requirements of the law of God, desires and determines to fulfill the requirements. But the law of sin in our members,
when it realizes that the law of good in our soul desires to
fulfill the holy and good requirements of the law of God outside of us, will surely oppose, resist, and usually overcome the
law of good in our soul. Thus, we are not only disabled from
fulfilling God's law, but instead we violate the holy and good
requirements of the law of God outside us. This is because the
law of sin in our body is stronger than the law of good in our
soul. However, the law of the Spirit of life in our spirit is even
stronger than the law of good in our soul. Therefore, if we
turn to our spirit and live according to our spirit, the law of
the Spirit of life in our spirit will deliver us from the law of
sin in our body and cause us to live out the divine life of God.
Thus, not only will we be able to fulfill the holy and good
requirements of God, but we can meet the divine standard of
God Himself.

For example, the outward law of God requires us not to be
covetous. The law of good in our soul, upon touching this
requirement of God's law, desires to fulfill it and determines
not to be covetous any more. But at this time the law of sin in
our body immediately rises in opposition, causing us to be
inwardly covetous; thus, we are unable to fulfill the law of
God which requires us not to be covetous. At this time, however much we will and determine, we cannot rid ourselves of a
covetous heart. On the contrary, the more we will and strive
to rid ourselves of covetousness, the more it grows within us.
Whenever, due to the outward requirement of God's law, the
law of good in our soul desires to do good, the law of sin in our
body will immediately cause evil to work in us and war
against our thought of good. Furthermore, the law of good in
our soul is no match for the law of sin in our body; in almost
every encounter it loses to the law of sin in our body. But,
praise the Lord, the law of the Spirit of life in our spirit is
stronger than the law of sin in our body and is able to deliver
us and set us free from the law of sin. If we would cease from
our struggling and strife through the law of good in our soul,
and walk instead according to the law of the Spirit of life, we

should be delivered from the covetous desire motivated by the law of sin in our body. We would be enabled to fulfill the requirement of the outward law of God not to covet and live out the surpassing holiness of God.

Hence we can see clearly that the outward law of God puts certain requirements upon us, and immediately the law of good in our soul desires to fulfill them. But the law of sin in our body between these two laws—the outward law of God and the law of good in our soul—obstructs and hinders us so that the law of good in our soul cannot fulfill the requirement of the outward law of God as it wishes. Just as our body surrounds our soul, so the law of sin in the body surrounds the law of good in our soul and is stronger than it. Therefore, it is very difficult for the law of good in our soul to overcome the law of sin in our body, to break through its surrounding and fulfill the requirement of the outward law of God. However, the law of the Spirit of life in our spirit is stronger than all; hence it can overcome the law of sin in our body and deliver us from the engulfing of that law, thus more than enabling us to fully fulfill the requirement of God's law.

We may use another illustration here to explain the relationship of these four laws to us. The outward law of God is like a respectable man proposing to us, while the law of good in our mind is like a virtuous lady saying yes to his proposal. However, the law of sin in our members is like a villain who always follows the lady and attempts to create trouble between her and that man. Whenever he observes this lady saying yes to the man's proposal, he kidnaps her and compels her to act neither according to her own will nor her own wish. At this very moment, the law of the Spirit of life in our spirit, which can be likened to an angel from heaven, rescues the lady from the villain and enables her to fulfill the man's proposal; thus, her desire is fulfilled. Consequently, she discovers that this angel from heaven is in fact the One whom the man represented. Therefore, this angel, by causing her to fulfill the man's proposal, actually enables her to fulfill his own desire.

From this illustration we see that although the outward law of God places requirements upon us, it cannot cause us to fulfill its requirements. The law of good in our mind desires to fulfill the requirements of the outward law of God, yet it has no strength to overcome the law of sin in our members. Moreover, the law of sin always opposes the law of good, and when it sees that the law of good is attempting to fulfill the requirement of the law of God, it will surely hinder and prevent it from fulfilling its wish. But the law of the Spirit of life in our spirit, our deliverance from God with the mighty power of the life of God, sets us free from the law of sin, thus enabling us to fulfill all the requirements of the law of God and live out the divine life of God. If we live according to this law of the Spirit of life, we shall be delivered from the law of sin in our members and become a victorious Christian automatically.

CONCLUSIONS

At this point we can draw several conclusions: First, God's deliverance differs from man's reformation. First of all, the basis is different. Man's reformation is based on the original good of man, while God's deliverance is based on the life of God and the Spirit of God, that is, the Spirit of life. Next, the methods differ. Man's reformation is by way of exerting human strength, inflicting harsh treatment on our body, and subduing the passions, thus bringing forth the good in man. God's deliverance is by way of putting His Spirit and His life into our spirit, thus quickening our spirit; then a renewing work begins from our spirit, renewing firstly the various parts of our spirit, then the different parts of our soul, and finally our physical body. Lastly, the results are different. The result of man's reformation is but the highest human excellence; it cannot cause man to live out the divine standard of God's nature. The consequence of God's deliverance is that we become God-men, living out the divine life of God.

Second, God's deliverance does not make us good men but life-men. There are all together three classes of man in the universe: God-men, good men, and evil men. God's deliverance is not to make us evil men or good men, but life-men.

Third, we who have been delivered by God ought to live in God. God is life, and God's deliverance is for us to become life-men. Life is God; to be a life-man is to be a God-man. To be such men we ought to live in God. But to live in God is a vague doctrine. If we want to live in God, we must live in the law of the Spirit of life. This requires us to live in spirit, for the law of the Spirit of life is in the spirit. This also requires us to live in the sense of life, for the sense of life is the sense of the law of the Spirit of life. If we obey the sense of life, we mind the spirit and live in the spirit. If we mind the spirit, we live in the law of the Spirit of life. When we live in the law of the Spirit of life, we live in God. Consequently, what we live out is God Himself. God is life; therefore, what we live out is life, and we become life-men.

Fourth, the goal of God's deliverance is the unity of God and man. When we obey the law of the Spirit of life and live in God, God lives also in us, and He and we mingle in a practical way until the two are completely united as one.

There are two more points on the subjective side. First, we must touch the inner sense, which means to obey the inner feeling. Second, we must live in fellowship. Fellowship is the flowing of life. To live in fellowship is to live in the flowing of life. These two points enable us to experience life in a practical way. The purpose of this chapter on the three lives and four laws is to bring us to this point. If we touch the inner sense in a practical way and live in fellowship, we will automatically be able: (1) to be freed from sin, (2) to do the good works which we are unable to do, (3) to fulfill the law of God, and (4) to live out the life of God. Eventually we can become God-men, manifesting the life of God. This is the goal of God's salvation, and this also includes all matters pertaining to life.

CHAPTER TEN

THE LAW OF LIFE

In the last chapter we have seen the three lives and four laws. Now we shall especially see the law of life, which is also the law of the Spirit of life mentioned in the last chapter. Of the four laws, only the law of life is the natural capability of the life of God, enabling us to live out the life of God quite naturally; therefore, if we want to touch the way of life, we must have clear knowledge concerning the law of life.

I. SCRIPTURAL BASIS

In the whole Bible, only the following five portions can be said to mention the law of life directly or indirectly:

A. Romans 8:2, *"the law of the Spirit of life..."*

The law of the Spirit of life mentioned here is the law of life. The Spirit, from which this law comes, contains life, or it may be said that it is life; therefore, the law is a law of the Spirit, and it is also the law of life.

B. Hebrews 8:10, *"This is the covenant that I will make with the house of Israel after those days, saith the Lord; I will put my laws into their mind, and on their heart also will I write them: and I will be to them a God, and they shall be to me a people."*

C. Hebrews 10:16, *"This is the covenant that I will make with them after those days, saith the Lord: I will put my laws on their heart, and upon their mind also will I write them."*

The above two passages in Hebrews 8 and 10 mention firstly "put," and then "write," and both speak of the mind and the heart; thus, both speak of the same thing. They are quoted from Jeremiah 31:33.

D. Jeremiah 31:33, *"This is the covenant that I will make*

with the house of Israel after those days, saith Jehovah: I will put my law in their inward parts, and in their heart will I write it; and I will be their God, and they shall be my people."

E. Ezekiel 36:25-28, *"I will sprinkle clean water upon you, and ye shall be clean: from all your filthiness, and from all your idols, will I cleanse you. A new heart also will I give you, and a new spirit will I put within you; and I will take away the stony heart out of your flesh, and I will give you a heart of flesh. And I will put my Spirit within you, and cause you to walk in my statutes, and ye shall keep mine ordinances, and do them...and ye shall be my people, and I will be your God."*

These few verses speak of at least five things: (1) cleansing with clean water, (2) giving us a new heart, (3) giving us a new spirit, (4) taking away our stony heart and giving us a heart of flesh, and (5) putting the Spirit of God within us. The result of these five combined together is that we are caused to walk in the statutes of God and to keep and do His ordinances. We shall be His people, and He shall be our God. This means that the Holy Spirit within us gives us new strength to do the will of God and to please God, so that God can be our God and we can be God's people. Thus, the result mentioned here is the same as the result mentioned in Jeremiah 31:33.

II. THE ORIGIN OF THE LAW OF LIFE— REGENERATION

If we wish to speak of the origin of the law of life, we must begin from regeneration, for regeneration is the receiving of God's life into our spirit. Once we are regenerated, we have the life of God in our spirit; and once we have the life of God, we naturally have the law of life which comes from the life of God.

A. The Creation of Man

When speaking of regeneration, we must begin with the creation of man. When man was created by the hand of God, he had only a good and upright human life; he did not have the divine and eternal life of God. Yet when God created man, His central purpose was to blend His life into man, to be united with man, and to reach the goal of the oneness of God and man. Therefore, when God created man, in addition to the body and soul of man, He especially created a spirit for man. This spirit is the organ by which man receives the life of God. When we use this spirit to contact God, who is a Spirit, we then can receive His life and become united with Him, thus fulfilling the central purpose of God.

B. The Fall of Man

But before man received the life of God, he fell. The most essential factor of the fall of man was not just that it caused him to commit sin and offend God, but that it caused his spirit to become deadened, or that it brought death to the organ by which man receives the life of God. To say that the spirit is dead does not mean that the spirit is nonexistent, but that it has lost its function to fellowship with God and has become separated from God; thus, man could no longer fellowship with God. Henceforth, man was unable to use his spirit to contact God and thereby receive His life.

At this time, man had needs on two sides: on one hand, because of the fall, he needed God to deal with the sin he committed; on the other hand, he needed God even more to regenerate him by giving life to his dead spirit, so that he might receive God's life and fulfill God's central purpose in creating man.

C. God's Way of Deliverance

Because of these needs, God's way of deliverance consists of two aspects, the negative and the positive. On the negative side, by the Lord Jesus shedding His blood on the cross, redemption was accomplished, and the problem of man's sin was settled. On the positive side, by the death of the Lord Jesus, the life of God was released; then by the resurrection of the Lord Jesus, the life of God was put in the Holy Spirit; eventually the Holy Spirit entering into us causes us to obtain God's divine and eternal life.

The Holy Spirit thus enabling us to obtain the life of God means that He regenerates us. But how does the Holy Spirit regenerate us? It is by the Word of God. The Holy Spirit first prepares an opportunity for us in our environment to hear the words of the Gospel. Then by the words, He shines upon us and moves us; He causes us to acknowledge our sins, reproach ourselves, repent and believe, thereby accepting the words of God and receiving the life of God. In the words of God is hidden the life of God, and the words of God "are life" (John 6:63). As we receive the words of God, the life of God enters into us and regenerates us.

Therefore, regeneration is nought else but the fact of man, in addition to his own life, receiving the life of God. When we thus receive the life of God, we receive an authority which enables us to become children of God (John 1:12). The authority itself is the life of God; therefore, when we have this life, we have the authority to be the children of God.

When we have the life of God and become children of God, we naturally have the divine nature (2 Pet. 1:4). If we live by this life and the nature of this life, we can become like God and live out the image of God.

How does the life of God within us work to make us become like Him? It works from the center to the circumference, or from the spirit to the soul and then to the body, accomplishing its outward expansion. When the life of God enters into us, it first enters into our spirit, quickens our dead spirit, and makes it lively, fresh, strong, vigorous, and able to touch God, sense God, and have sweet fellowship with God. Then it spreads gradually from our spirit into every part of our soul and makes our thoughts, affections, and decisions gradually become like God's, having the savor of God; even in our anger, there is something of God's likeness, something of the savor of God. Oh, what a wonderful change this is!

Furthermore, this life will work continuously until it expands into our body, so that our body also may have the life element. This is what Romans 8:11 speaks of: the Spirit of God which dwells in us can quicken our mortal bodies.

The life of God within us will work and expand more and more until it causes our spirit, soul, and body, or our whole being, to be completely filled with the nature of God, the element of God, and the savor of God; until we are raptured and transfigured; until we enter into glory and become completely like Him.

The life of God continuously working and expanding within us does not force its way through by ignoring us; rather it requires the inclination of our emotion, the cooperation of our mind, and the submission of our will. If we refuse its working, if we do not follow it closely and cooperate with it, it has no way to show forth its power or manifest its function. Because man is a living being with affection, mind, and will, the question of whether he will cooperate and whether he can cooperate remains a problem. Hence, when God regenerates us, besides giving us His life, He also gives us a new heart and puts within us a new spirit (Ezek. 36:26); thus, we are made both willing and able to cooperate.

The heart has to do with our willingness, while the spirit is a matter of capability. Our original heart, because of rebellion against God, became hard or old; therefore, it is called a "stony heart" or an "old heart." This old heart is against God, does not want God, and is not willing to cooperate with God. Now God gives us a new heart. It is not that He gives us another heart in addition to our old heart, but that through the regeneration of the Holy Spirit He softens our stony heart to become a "heart of flesh," thus renewing it to become a new heart. This new heart is inclined toward God and has affection for God and the things of God. It is a new organ for inclining toward God and loving Him; it makes us willing to cooperate with God and willing to allow the life of God to expand and work freely from inside to outside.

The spirit we originally had, because of separation from God, is dead and has become old; therefore, it is called an "old spirit." Since this old spirit has lost its ability to fellowship with God and contact God, it naturally has no way to cooperate with God. Now God gives us a "new spirit." This does not mean that He gives us another spirit in addition to our old spirit, but that by the regeneration of the Holy Spirit He quickens our dead spirit into a living spirit, thus renewing it into a new spirit. This new spirit can fellowship with God and can apprehend God and spiritual things. It is a new organ for contacting God; it enables us to cooperate with God and, through fellowshipping with God, to allow the life of God within us to expand and work outward.

With a new heart we are *willing* to cooperate with God, and with a new spirit we are *able* to cooperate with God. However, a new heart and a new spirit at most only enable us to thirst after God and contact God, thus allowing the life of God within us to freely expand and work outward; they cannot answer the unlimited demand of God upon us, which is that we reach the divine standard of God Himself. Therefore, when God regenerates us, He does in addition a most glorious and transcendent thing: He puts His own Spirit, the Holy Spirit, into our new spirit. This Holy Spirit is the embodiment of Christ, and Christ in turn is the embodiment of God. Therefore, the Holy Spirit entering into us is the Triune God entering into us. In this way the Creator and the creature are united. Oh, this truly deserves our praise! Moreover, the Spirit of God, the eternal Spirit or the infinite Spirit, has unlimited functions and transcendent strength. Hence, when He dwells in our new spirit, He can use His unlimited power to anoint and supply us, to work and move within us; thus, He enables us to answer the unlimited demand of God upon us, thereby allowing the life of God to expand continually from our spirit, through our soul, and into our body. Finally, He causes us to reach that glorious stage of being completely like God! Hallelujah!

One thing is clearly revealed to us here: God's way of deliverance and man's self-improvement are fundamentally different. Man's self-improvement is but a work wrought upon that which man originally has, namely his soul and his body with their capabilities. Even if the improvement is successful, it is still very limited because the power of man is limited. But, with the deliverance of God, though it also passes through every part of our soul and gradually renews each one, reaching also into the body, the essential point is that the Spirit of God, bringing with it the life of God, is added into our spirit. Having divine, unlimited power, it is fully able to answer the unlimited demand of God. This is an addition, not an improvement. To attempt improvement is but to improve the things we already have, and this is limited; but to add something of God Himself is unlimited.

What we have just said should make us see clearly that regeneration causes us to receive the life of God. In this life is contained a natural function, and the natural function of this life is the "law of life." Thus, the life of God is the source of this law of life, and regeneration is the origin of this law of life. Though this law of life is derived from the life of God, yet it is through regeneration that it enters into us.

III. THE MEANING OF THE LAW OF LIFE

If we would know the meaning of the law of life, we must know what a law is. A law is a natural regulation, a constant and unchanging rule. A law is not necessarily derived from a life, but a life is definitely accompanied by a law. This law which accompanies life is called the law of life. The law of a particular life is also the natural characteristic, the innate function, of that particular life. For example, cats can catch mice, and dogs can stand watch for the night; or, our ear can hear, our nose can smell, our tongue can taste, and our stomach can digest. All these abilities are the natural characteristics and innate functions of a life. As long as any particular life exists and is free, it can naturally develop its characteristics and manifest its abilities. It does not require human teaching or urging; rather it develops very naturally without the least effort. Such natural characteristics and innate capabilities in a life constitute the law of that life.

The life of God is the highest life; it is the surpassing life; therefore, the characteristics and capabilities of this life must definitely be the most high and surpassing. Since these highest and surpassing characteristics and capabilities constitute the law of the life of God, this law naturally is the most high and surpassing. Since by regeneration we have received the life of God, we have naturally received from the life of God the most high and surpassing law of this life.

In the first chapter, *What Is Life?*, we said that only the life of God is life; therefore, the law of life of which we are now speaking refers specifically to the law of the life of God.

The law of life is that which God specially gives to us

under the new covenant. It is very different from the laws given by God at Mt. Sinai. In the Old Testament time, God gave a law written on tablets of stone outside of man's body. That law was an external law, a law of letters. It made demands upon man outwardly, rule by rule, requiring what man should do and what he should not do. But the result was nil; no one could keep it. Though the law was good, yet man being evil and dead did not have the power of life to meet the demands of that law. On the contrary, he fell under the condemnation of that law. Romans 8:3 refers to this when it says: "What the law could not do, in that it was weak through the flesh..."

In the New Testament era, when God through the Holy Spirit regenerates us, He puts His own life, accompanied by the law of life, into us. This law of life is the inward law which is God's special gift to us in the New Testament time. This fulfills the promise of God written in the Old Testament, "I will put my law in their inward parts" (Jer. 31:33).

This law of life is put within us; therefore, according to its location, it is an inward law. It is not like the law of the Old Testament which was outside of man and was therefore an outward law. Furthermore, this law of life is derived from the life of God and belongs to the life of God; therefore, according to its nature, it is a law of life; hence it can supply. It is not like the law of the Old Testament, which is a law of letters, and which can only demand but cannot supply. This law of life in us, this law which is the natural characteristic and capability of the life of God, is able very naturally to regulate out item by item all the content within the life of God. The result of this regulating perfectly answers the demand of the outward law of God.

Let us use two examples to illustrate how the law of life functions. Consider a withered peach tree. Suppose we set up some laws for it, demanding: "You must grow out green leaves, bloom red flowers, and bear peaches." We know that such demands, though made from the beginning of the year till the end of the year, are absolutely futile and vain, because the tree is withered with no power of life to answer the demands of such outward laws. Yet if we could transfuse life

into it and restore it to life though we do not demand anything outwardly from it, that life will have a natural
capability which will enable the tree to grow leaves, flower,
and bear fruit in season, even to exceed the demand of that
outward law. This is the function of the law of life.

Suppose now that we make demands on a dead man,
saying: "You should breathe; you should eat; you should sleep;
you should move." We know that the demands of such laws
upon this dead man are of no effect at all; none of them can be
fulfilled. Yet if we could put resurrection life into him and
bring him back to life, he will very naturally want to breathe,
eat, sleep, and move. This is due to the function of the law of
life.

From these two examples we can clearly see that our
entire spiritual life before God cannot be accomplished by our
own striving; neither can it be achieved by self-improvement
with utmost effort; rather, it is the responsibility of the life of
God which we have already received into us. The life of God
accompanied by the law of this life dwells in our spirit; if we
live and act according to this law of life in our spirit, this law
of life can very naturally regulate out from within us, item by
item, all the content within the life of God. This will correspond very well with the demand of the external law of God,
and even exceed it with no deficiency. Romans 8:4 speaks of
this: "That the righteous requirement of the law might be fulfilled in us, who do walk not according to the flesh but
according to the Spirit."

This law of life written on the tablet of the heart within us
is called "the law of the Spirit of life" in Romans 8:2. This
means that this law is not only from the life of God and
belongs to the life of God, but it also depends on the Spirit of
God and belongs to the Spirit of God. This is because the life
of God relies on the Spirit of God, and the Spirit of God can
also be said to be the life of God. When we speak of the life of
God, we are stressing that which is itself the life of God; when
we speak of the Spirit of God, we are emphasizing the executor of the life of God. In other words, the life of God is not a
person, but the Spirit of God is a person. This life which is not
a person belongs to the Spirit, who is a person, and cannot be

separated from this Spirit, who is a person. This Spirit, who is a person, brings the life of God into us; and this life is accompanied by a law, which is the law of life, or the law of the Spirit of life. This law has the eternal life of God as its source, and this law has the Spirit of God, who is a person with great power, as its executor. Therefore, this law of the Spirit of life has eternal and unlimited power to answer the unlimited demand of God.

Thus, we have seen that the law of the Old Testament is the law of letters written on tablets of stone. Though it made many demands upon man, the result was nil. The law of the New Testament is the law of life written on the tablet of our heart. Even though it would not make any demand upon us, yet in the end it can naturally regulate out from us all the riches of God, thus making us more than able to answer all the demands of God. How wonderful and how glorious this is! This is the central grace which God gives us in the New Covenant! How much we should thank and praise Him!

IV. THE SEAT OF THE LAW OF LIFE

A. The Seat of the Working of the Law of Life

The life from which issues the law of life is the life of God. When at our regeneration we first receive this life, this life within us, though it is complete organically, is not grown up and mature in each individual part of our whole being. It is like fruit borne on a tree. The life of this fruit when it first appears, though it is complete, is only complete organically. For it to be complete in every part, it must wait until it is grown and mature. Likewise, the life of God we receive at the time of regeneration is only complete organically. If we want this life to have completion of maturity, it also needs to gradually grow and mature in every part of our whole being. The growing and maturing of this life comes about by the working of the law of life in every part of our whole being. This reveals that the place where the law of life works is in every part of our whole being. This is what Jeremiah 31:33 refers to as our "inward parts."

B. The Inward Parts and Laws

What are our inward parts? These are the parts of our spirit, soul, and heart. This heart is not the *biological* heart, but the *psychological* heart. Within us human beings, the spirit and the soul are independent parts, but the heart is of a composite nature. According to the record in the Bible, the heart contains at least:

1. The mind. For example: "think ye evil in your hearts" (Matt. 9:4), and "thoughts of the heart" (Heb. 4:12).

2. The will. For example: "with purpose of heart" (Acts 11:23), and "intents of the heart" (Heb. 4:12).

3. The emotion. For example: "Let not your heart be troubled" (John 14:1), and "your heart shall rejoice" (John 16:22).

4. The conscience. For example: "having our heart... an evil conscience" (Heb. 10:22), and "if our heart condemns" (1 John 3:20).

These references show us that the heart contains the mind, will, and emotion, which are the three parts of the soul, and the conscience, which is a part of the spirit. The heart has these parts as its components. Thus, the heart not only consists of a component of the spirit and all the components of the soul, but it really connects the spirit and soul together.

Of the various parts within us, the intuition and fellowship parts of the spirit are more related to God and are for God; the conscience part in the spirit, having the power to discern between right and wrong, is more related to man and is for man. The mind, will, and emotion in the soul, being the seat of the personality of man, are also more for man and related to man's side. Since the heart contains the mind, emotion, will, and conscience, it is thus a composite part which brings together these various inward parts of man. It can be considered as man's chief representative.

The law of life within us continuously works in these various inward parts. Whichever part its work reaches, it becomes the law of that part. When its work reaches the mind, it becomes the law of the mind. When its work reaches the will, it becomes the law of the will. When its work reaches the emotion, it becomes the law of the emotion. When its work reaches the conscience, it becomes the law of the conscience. In this way, it becomes a law to each of our inward parts. Thus Hebrews 8:10 and 10:16 name this law, "laws." These "laws" actually are but the one inward law, which is the law of life, or what God speaks of as "law" in Jeremiah 31:33; but it is put in the various "parts" within us.

In Jeremiah this law of life is called "law," while in Hebrews it is called "laws"—one is singular, and the other plural. This is because when speaking of the law itself, there is only one; therefore, it is singular. Yet when speaking of the effects of the working of this law, since it manifests its capabilities and functions in the various parts of our whole being, it becomes various laws; therefore, it is plural. Whether Jeremiah calls it the singular law or Hebrews calls it the plural laws, they both really refer to this one law.

C. The Relationship between the Heart and the Law of Life

We have seen that the place where the law of life works is in our various inward parts. Of these various parts, the heart is the chief. This is because the heart is the conglomerate of man's inward parts, and it is man's chief representative. Therefore, the heart is very closely related to the law of life, which works in our various inward parts and thereby becomes the various laws. For this reason, we shall speak in detail of the situation of the heart.

1. The Heart Is the Entrance and Exit of Life

We have already mentioned that the heart connects the spirit and the soul; thus, the heart is in between the spirit and the soul. If life is to enter into the spirit, it must pass through the heart; if life is to proceed out from the spirit, it also must pass through the heart. Thus, the heart is the pathway through which life must pass. It can be said to be the entrance and exit of life. For example, when someone hears the Gospel of the Lord and feels the pain and sorrow of sin or the sweetness of God's love, the emotion of his heart is touched, his conscience is grieved, his mind repents, and his will determines to believe. Then his heart is opened to the Lord, he receives salvation, and the life of God thereby enters into his spirit. Conversely, if his heart does not agree and is not open, regardless of how you preach to him, there is no way for the life of God to enter into his spirit. It is for this reason that the great British evangelist, Mr. Spurgeon, once said that in order to move man's spirit, one must move man's heart. This statement is really true; only when the heart is moved can the spirit receive the life of God.

Likewise, after man is saved, if the life of God is to come out from within him, it must pass through the heart and have the cooperation of the heart. When the heart agrees, life can pass through. When the heart does not agree, life cannot pass through. Sometimes the heart only partially agrees. Perhaps only the conscience agrees, and other parts do not. Or, perhaps the mind of the heart agrees, while the emotion part does not. Hence, life still cannot pass through. Thus, the heart is really the entrance and exit of life. Just as the receiving of life begins with the heart, so also the living out of life begins with the heart.

2. The Heart Is the Switch of Life

The heart is the entrance and exit of life: the coming in of life and the going out of life both depend on the heart. Moreover, the heart is also the switch of life. If the heart is shut, life can neither enter in nor be regulated out. Once the heart is open, however, life can enter in and also be freely regulated out. Whichever part of the heart is closed, the life of God cannot regulate to that part; whichever part of the heart is open, the life of God can regulate to that part. Thus, the heart is really the switch of life. Though life has great power, yet its great power is controlled by our small heart. Whether life can be worked out depends entirely on whether our heart is open. It is like the electric power of a generating plant, which, though powerful, is controlled by the small switch for the light in our room; if the switch is not turned on, electricity cannot enter.

This does not mean, of course, that as long as we have a proper heart it is sufficient. The heart can only cause us to love God and be inclined toward God; it cannot make us touch God and have fellowship with God. It is the spirit that causes us to touch God and have fellowship with God. This is why many brothers and sisters, though they love the Lord very much, cannot touch God in prayer. They have a heart, but they do not use the spirit. Many revivalists fail in their work for the same reason. They only move man's emotion, stir man's will, and make men love God and be desirous of God; they do not guide men to exercise their spirit to fellowship with God.

It is true that in order to understand spiritual things we need to use the mind of the heart, yet we must first use the spirit to contact these things, for the spirit is the organ to contact the spiritual world. We must first contact all spiritual things by the spirit, then comprehend and understand them with the mind of the heart. It is like hearing sound: it is first contacted with the ear and then comprehended by the mind. It is also like beholding a certain color: it must first be contacted with the eyes and then distinguished with the mind. Therefore, when we preach the Gospel to men, if our spirit is weak, we only use words to cause people to comprehend and understand with their mind; later we may lead them to touch the Spirit. When our spirit is strong, however, we send God's salvation directly into men's spirit by the words of the Gospel. As soon as men hear the Gospel, they touch the spirit and are saved. After that we gradually lead their mind to comprehend and understand.

Though the main function in contacting God and spiritual things is the exercise of the spirit, yet if man's heart is indifferent, the spirit is then imprisoned within and is unable to show forth its capability. Even if God wants to fellowship and commune with him, it is impossible. Therefore, in order to contact God and spiritual things, we need to use the spirit, and we also need to have the heart so inclined. The spirit is the organ to contact the life of God, and the heart is the key, the switch, the strategic point which allows the life of God to pass through.

3. The Heart Can
Hinder the Working of Life

Since the heart is the entrance and exit of life and the switch of life as well, it has great influence on life; its slightest problem can fully hinder the working of life. Whichever part of the heart has a problem, life is obstructed and brought to a standstill there, and the law of life cannot regulate any more.

The life of God within us should be able to freely work and grow, causing us to receive daily revelation and frequent light. This is normal and is also fitting. But actually this is often not the case. There are many brothers and sisters whose spiritual life does not grow and whose spiritual living is not normal. It is not because the life of God in them is unreal; neither is it because there is any problem with the life of God within them; it is their heart which has trouble. Their heart is not turned sufficiently toward God, it does not love the Lord enough, it does not seek the Lord enough, it is not clean enough, and it is not sufficiently open. This reveals some trouble or problem with the heart. Either there is some problem with the conscience, which has the sense of condemnation but is not dealt with, or there is a problem with the mind concerning some care, worry, evil thought, argument, or doubt, etc. Either there is a problem with the will being stubborn and stiff-necked, or there is a problem with the emotion having fleshly desires and natural inclination. All these matters in the heart become a hindrance to the working of the life within us, making it impossible for the law of life to regulate. Therefore, if we desire to grow in life, we need first to deal with the heart, and then to exercise the spirit. If the heart is not dealt with, there is no point in mentioning the spirit. The problem of many brothers and sisters is not with the spirit but with the heart. If the heart is not right, then life in the spirit is hindered, and the law of life cannot work freely. If we desire to seek after life and walk in the path of life, we must have no problem in the heart; then the law of life can work freely and move without obstruction, thereby reaching every part of our whole being.

4. How to Deal with the Heart

Since the heart is so vitally related to life, God has no other alternative but to deal with our heart that His life might be regulated out from us. Toward God, our heart has four great problems: hardness, impurity, unlovingness, and unpeacefulness. Hardness is a matter of the will, impurity is a matter not only of the mind but also of the emotion, unlovingness is a matter of the emotion, and unpeacefulness is a matter of the conscience. When God deals with our heart, He deals with these four aspects so that our heart may be soft, pure, loving, and at peace.

Firstly, God wants our heart to be soft. To be soft means that the will of the heart toward God is submissive and yielding, not stiff-necked and rebellious. When God deals with our heart so that our heart is soft, He takes away the stony heart out of our flesh and gives us a heart of flesh (Ezek. 36:26). This means that He softens our hard, stony heart so that it becomes a soft heart of flesh.

When we are newly saved, the heart is always softened. But after a certain time, the heart of some turns back and becomes hard again. Not being submissive to the Lord and not even fearing the Lord, they gradually fall away from the Lord's presence. Whenever our heart is hardened, we have a problem before God. If we desire the condition of our spiritual living before God to be right, our heart must not be hardened; on the contrary, it must be continually softened. Indeed we should not be fearful of this thing and that thing, but we ought to be fearful of offending God. Fear not heaven, and fear not earth; only fear to offend God. Our heart must be dealt with until it is soft to this extent; then it is all right. It is indeed sad that many brothers and sisters are soft in many things; yet as soon as God and the will of God are mentioned, they become very hard. They would even say: "I am just this way; let us see what God will do about it." This is dreadful! There are also brothers and sisters who are hard toward everything; yet when God and the will of God are mentioned, they become soft. Such people have soft hearts. We should ask God to make our heart soft like this.

How does God make our heart soft? How does He soften our heart? Sometimes He uses His love to move us, and sometimes He uses chastisement to strike us. God often uses His love first to move us; if love cannot move us, He uses His hand through the environment to strike us until our heart is softened. Once our heart is softened, His life can work within us.

Secondly, God wants our heart to be pure. A pure heart means a heart that sets its mind specifically on God. It is also a heart in which the emotion is exceedingly pure and simple toward God. (See 2 Cor. 11:3.) It only loves God and wants God; besides God, it has no other love, inclination, or desire. Matthew 5:8 says: "the pure in heart...shall see God." Thus, if the heart is not pure, we cannot see God. If our thought is a little concerned with things outside of God, or if our emotion has a little love toward things outside of God, our heart is no longer pure; the life in our spirit is also hindered because of this. Therefore, we must pursue "with them that call on the Lord out of a pure heart" (2 Tim. 2:22), and be those who love the Lord and want God with a pure heart; then we can let the life of God work freely within us.

Thirdly, God wants our heart to be loving. A loving heart means a heart in which the emotion loves God, wants God, thirsts after God, yearns for God, and has affection toward God. In the Bible, there is a book which speaks specifically of the love of the saints toward the Lord—The Song of Songs in the Old Testament. It says there that as the Lord's people we should love the Lord as a woman loves her beloved. This love is so deep and unchanging and is stronger than death (8:6-7). Because this book speaks especially of our love toward the Lord, it also shows forth especially our growth in the life of the Lord. Then in the New Testament, in John chapter twenty-one, the Lord asked Peter three times: "Lovest thou me?" This means that the Lord desired to lead the emotion of Peter to so love the Lord that he could be one who has a loving heart toward the Lord. The Lord did this because He wanted Peter to afford His life an opportunity to work and grow within him. This event is recorded in the Gospel of John, a book which speaks of how we may receive the Lord as life and how to live in this life. If our heart has such love toward the

Lord, the life of the Lord within us can move smoothly and do as it pleases.

Fourthly, God wants our heart to be at peace. A heart at peace means a heart in which the conscience has no offense (Acts 24:16), no condemnation or reproach; it is safe and secure. The conscience within us represents God to govern us. If our conscience condemns us, God is greater than our conscience and knows all things (1 John 3:20); He would even condemn us more. Thus, we must deal clearly with all the offenses, condemnation, and reproach; so we "shall assure our heart before him" (1 John 3:19). When our heart is thus at peace, God can pass through, and the law of the life of God can continue to work within us.

If our heart is soft, pure, loving, and at peace, it is then upright. Only such an upright heart is a suitable counterpart to the law of life. It can allow the life of God to be freely regulated out from within us. How often toward God our heart seems to carry a sign: "Not a through street"; thus, we make it impossible for God to pass through; we cause the life of God to become obstructed and come to a standstill, so that it is unable to work and expand freely from within us to without.

Though these words are not of great eloquence and wisdom, yet they should make us carefully examine, as in a physical examination, all the conditions of our heart. We must ask ourselves, Does the will of our heart really choose God? Is it submissive and surrendered before God? Or is it stiff-necked and rebellious? We also should ask, Is the mind of our heart pure before God? Or is it crooked? Our thoughts, our cares—are they purely for God Himself? Or is there outside of God a person, a matter, or a thing which we are deeply concerned for and which has occupied our heart? Then we need to ask, Is the emotion of our heart single toward God? Does it love God and want God wholly? Or does it have some other love, some other inclination, some other attachment outside of God? We also should ask, How is our conscience before God? Is it without offense? Is it assured? Or does it have condemnation and reproach? We should carefully examine all these items and deal with them carefully, so that our heart may become a soft heart, a pure heart, a loving heart, and a peaceful heart—in other words, an upright heart. If so, the life in our spirit will definitely have a way out, and the law of life can definitely be regulated out from within us.

Thus, in whatever part our heart has been dealt with, there the life of God can work, and there the law of the life of God can also regulate. When all parts of our heart are examined and dealt with, the law of the life of God can then regulate out from our spirit through our heart to every part of our whole being. Hence, every part of our whole being can manifest the capability of this law of life and be filled with the element of the life of God, thereby reaching the glorious end of the unity of God and man.

V. REQUIREMENTS OF THE LAW OF LIFE

Since we have seen the seat of the law of life, we know that this law of life works in the various inward parts of our whole being. Yet in actual practice, if the law of life is to work freely in our various inward parts, we need to fulfill two requirements:

A. Love God

The first requirement is to love God. The Gospel of John speaks especially of life; it also speaks emphatically of belief and love. To believe is to take in life, while to love is to flow out life. If we want to receive life, we must believe. If we want to live out life, we must love. Only belief can allow life to enter in, and only love can allow life to flow out. Therefore, love is a necessary condition which enables the law of life to work.

In another place we see that the Bible wants us to love God with all our heart, all our soul, all our mind, and all our strength (Mark 12:30). When we love God to such an extent that we allow our love for God to reach the many parts within us, the life of God can begin to function and regulate in these many parts within us. Thus, these parts gradually become like God.

Thus, God first sows His life within us; then He uses love to move the emotion of our heart and cause our heart to love Him, turn toward Him and become attached to Him. In this way the veil within us is taken away (see 2 Cor. 3:16), and we can see light, receive revelation, and know God and the life of God. Furthermore, when we love God with all our heart, we are naturally willing to submit to God and cooperate with God. In this way we allow the law of the life of God to freely work within us and supply every part of our entire being with all the riches of the life of God. Whichever part is filled with love for God, in the same part the law of the life of God then regulates. If our whole being loves God, the law of the life of God then works through our whole being. Then our entire being, both within and without, will become like God and be filled with the riches of the life of God.

B. Obey the First Sense of Life

The second requirement is to obey the first sense of life. In chapter seven, *The Sense of the Spirit and Knowing the Spirit,* we mentioned that the law of life belongs to consciousness; it can give us a sense. As soon as we are regenerated and have the life of God, this law of life inside us definitely causes us to have a certain consciousness. Our responsibility is to obey the sense of the law of life, thus allowing this law of life to freely work within us.

Nevertheless, in the beginning, the consciousness of this law of life may be comparatively weak and infrequent. Yet if only we are willing to obey the first sense, though it be comparatively weak, the consciousnesses following will be stronger and stronger. We just have to begin by submitting to this first weak consciousness and continue to submit. In this way the law of life can work within us unceasingly until it reaches the various inward parts of our whole being. Thus, the life within us will be enabled to expand outward very naturally and to increase in depth and height.

Some may ask, After we obey the first consciousness, what should we do next? Our answer is this: Before we obey the first sense, let us not be concerned about what we should do after that. God only gives us one consciousness at a time, just as God only gives us one day at a time. As we live day by day, so we obey the senses, one by one. When God gives us one consciousness, we simply obey this one consciousness. When we have obeyed this first consciousness, God naturally will give us the second consciousness. When God called Abraham, He only told him the first step: "Get thee out of thy country, and from thy kindred, and from thy father's house." After leaving these, what he should do and where he should go would be shown to him. God said, "I will show thee" (Gen. 12:1). When the Lord Jesus was born and King Herod sought to destroy Him, God only told Joseph the first step, which was to escape to Egypt; he was to be there *until* God would bring him word for the next step (Matt. 2:13).

This shows us that the reason God only gives us one consciousness at a time is that He wants us to look unto Him step by step and depend on Him moment by moment, thereby submitting unto Him. Therefore, the sense of the law of life is in the same principle as the tree of life—the principle of dependence. It makes us dependent upon God, that is, dependent upon God to give us one consciousness after another consciousness. It is not depending on Him only once, but depending on Him continuously. It is unlike the principle of the tree of the knowledge of good and evil, which is independence from God. Thus, every one of us who desires to live by the law of life must regard the first sense of life as important and obey it, and then continue to obey thereafter.

The law of life sometimes also gives us negative feelings. That is, when we take some action which is against God, which is not in harmony with the life of God, the law of life causes us to feel uneasy and insecure, and to have the taste of death. This is the being "forbidden" and the "suffering not" of God within us (Acts 16:6, 7). No matter what we want to do or what we are doing, as soon as we have such a sense of forbidding within us, we should stop. If we are able to move or stop according to the consciousness of the law of life within, this law of life can then work within us without hindrance; the life within us can also grow and expand continuously. Therefore, obeying the consciousness of the law of life—especially the first consciousness—is also a very vital condition for the law of life to work within us. The reason the apostle in Philippians 2 wants us to obey with fear and trembling is for God to work within us (vv. 12-13). The working of God within us requires our cooperation through obedience; therefore, our obedience becomes a requirement for the working of God.

VI. THE FUNCTION OF THE LAW OF LIFE

We have seen that love and obedience are the two requirements for the working of the law of life. They are also our two responsibilities toward the law of life. If we are able to love and willing to obey, the law of life can spontaneously work in the various parts within us and manifest its natural function.

There are two kinds of functions of the law of life. One is to take away or to kill, and the other is to add or to supply. On the one hand it takes away what we should not have in us, and on the other hand it adds in what we should have in us. What is taken away is the element of Adam in us, and what is added is the element of Christ as the life-giving Spirit. What is taken away is old, and what is added is new. What is taken away is dead, and what is added is living. When the law of life works within us, it has these two kinds of functions manifest within us: one is to gradually take away all of our old creation, and the other is to gradually add all of God's new creation. In this way, the life within us gradually comes up.

The reason the law of life within us can have these two kinds of functions is that the life from which this law is derived has two special elements: one is the element of death, and the other is the element of life. The element of death is that wonderful death of the Lord Jesus on the cross, that death which includes all and ends all. The element of life is the resurrection of the Lord Jesus, or the life of the resurrection power of the Lord; hence it is also called the element of resurrection.

The function of taking away in the law of life is derived from the element of the Lord's all-inclusive death contained in the life; therefore, just as the Lord's death on the cross eliminated all the difficulties which God found in man, so also today, through the working of the law of life, His death is being executed within us. It kills and takes away one by one all that which is not in harmony with God and which is outside of God, such as the element of sin, the element of the world, the element of the flesh, the element of lust, the element of the old creation, and the element of the natural constitution. The function of adding which is in the law of life is derived from the element of the Lord's resurrection contained in the life; therefore, just as the Lord's resurrection brought man into God, enabling man to participate in all of God Himself, so also today, through the working of the law of life, His resurrection is being applied within us. This means that it adds into us and supplies us with God's power, God's holiness, God's love, God's patience, and all the elements of God or the elements of the new creation, that we may be filled with all the fullness of the Godhead.

It is like the medicine we take, some of which contains two kinds of elements: the element to kill the germs and the element to nourish. The function of the killing element takes away the sickness which we should not have; the function of the nourishing element supplies the life elements we need.

It is also like the blood in our body, which contains two kinds of elements: the white blood corpuscles and the red blood corpuscles. White blood corpuscles have one function, to kill germs; the red blood corpuscles also have one function, to supply nourishment. When the blood circulates and flows within us, the white blood corpuscles kill and clean up the germs which have invaded our body, while the red blood corpuscles supply every part of our entire body with needed nourishment. Likewise, when the law of the life of God works within us, or when the life of God works within us, the two elements, life and death, contained in the life of God have the functions of killing and supplying within us—that is, killing our spiritual germs, such as the world and the flesh, and supplying us the spiritual nourishment, which consists of all the riches of God Himself.

Thus, we should see that here is a correct way for the pursuit of the growth in life. As soon as we are saved and have the life of God, the law of the life of God in us causes us to have a certain consciousness. If we want to seek growth in life, we have to love God and obey this consciousness to deal with the conscience, and to deal with the emotion, the thoughts, and the will. By having these dealings, the life of God in our spirit will continue to give us a certain consciousness. When we obey these feelings, the law of life will then regulate within us and manifest its two functions: taking away that which is outside of God and adding in all that is God Himself. In this way we can gradually grow and mature in the life of God. These are very real and practical experiences. The way of life we are speaking of lies here!

VII. THE POWER OF THE LAW OF LIFE

Besides the two functions mentioned above, the law of life also has power. We have already mentioned that the law of the Old Testament is the law written outside of man, the dead law, the law of letters. It only makes demands on man; it has no power to supply man so that he can answer its demands. Therefore, it "could not do" (Rom. 8:3), and it also "made nothing perfect" (Heb. 7:19). But the law of the New Testament is the law written in our inward parts, the living law, the law of life. This life is "the indestructible life" of God, which has "power" (Heb. 7:16). Thus, the law which comes from this life also has power, and it can enable us in all things.

We should see here that the power of the law of life is the power of the life of God from which the law comes. It was this power which enabled the Lord Jesus to rise from death and ascend to heaven, far above all. It is also this power which seeks to regulate within us every day and is able to do exceeding abundantly above all that we ask or think (Eph. 1:20; 3:20). This power can accomplish the following things within us:

A. It Can Incline Our Heart toward God

Firstly, this power can incline our heart toward God. When we spoke of the relationship between the law of life and the heart, we mentioned that the law of life can be hindered by the heart. If our heart is not inclined toward God, the life of God cannot pass through. But, thank God, His life within us does not just stop there. It will still continue to work within us to such a degree that our heart which is not inclined toward God becomes inclined toward God. Proverbs 21:1 says: "The king's heart is in the hand of Jehovah as the watercourses: he turneth it whithersoever he will." Thus, we can ask God, "Incline my heart unto thy testimonies, and not to covetousness" (Psa. 119:36). When we are willing to ask in this way, the power of the law of life of God can very naturally turn our heart back and make our heart completely inclined toward God.

B. It Can Make Us Submissive toward God

Secondly, this power can make us submissive toward God. When we spoke of the requirements of the law of life, we also mentioned that the working of the law of life in us requires our submission to match it. Yet how many times we not only cannot submit, but we even do not want to submit. At such times, the power of the law of life is fully able to deal with our condition to make us submissive.

Though we who are saved and have the life of God sometimes backslide and our heart becomes hardened and unable to obey God, God is merciful to us in that His life within us will not stop its regulating work. By His power, He regulates our emotion and regulates our will; thus, regulating to and fro He enables us to obey Him again.

Philippians 2:13 says that the matter of our will before God is also due to the working of God within us. Thus, the submission of our will is also the outcome of the working of the power of the law of God's life within us. This power can turn our disobedient will to be obedient to God.

Once there was a sister who felt she really could not obey. Not only was her mind disturbed, but her conscience also suffered accusation. She then asked God to rescue her. When she cried to God, God showed her the light in Philippians 2:13. She then knew that God could work to make her obedient. Thus, she was cheered and found rest.

C. It Can Cause Us to Do the Good Work God Has Ordained for Us

Thirdly, this power can also make us do the good works which God has afore prepared that we should walk in them (Eph. 2:10). Such good is from God, and flows out from the life of God; therefore, to do such good works is to live out God Himself. Such good, which far exceeds the good of man, can never be lived out by the human life. But the life of God within us, regulating us with His power, can cause us to live out such extraordinary good.

D. It Can Make Us Labor
with All Our Heart and Strength

Fourthly, this power can make us work for the Lord with all our heart and strength. The apostle Paul said that the reason he could labor more abundantly than other apostles was not due to himself, but to the grace of God bestowed upon him, or the grace of the life of God which was with him (1 Cor. 15:10). He also said that he labored, striving according to God's working which worked in him "in power" (Col. 1:29). The word "power" can also be translated as "dynamite." This means that his work was not dependent on his own soulish power, but on the dynamic power of the life of God which dwelt in him. In all past generations, those who were used by the Lord toiled continuously and suffered constantly in the work of the Lord. They labored not out of their individual striving, but because they loved God and inclined toward God, so that they allowed the life of God to work within them, to regulate within them, and to regulate out of them an activity, exploding out a work. This regulated-out activity or exploded-out work is the working out of the dynamic power of the life of God. When this dynamic power of the life of God regulates man from within, no one can remain inactive. Everyone who allows the dynamic power of the law of the life of God to work within him will definitely work with all his strength, measuring not his own life in any labor.

After the Sino-Japanese War, we went to work in several local churches. We were quite blessed and had much fruit. When we returned to Shanghai, Brother Nee said to me: "Brother, we are 'troublemakers.' We have just made trouble in other churches, and now we are going to make trouble in the church in Shanghai." Though these were humorous words, yet, seriously speaking, all who live in the life of God and allow the law of the life of God to work are definitely "troublemakers." This is because the life of God within them is an endless and powerful life, a positive and motivating life, a life with dynamic power. Whenever this life works and regulates within them, they will explode inside; they will carry out the work which has the dynamic power. Consequently, they naturally become troublemakers. Conversely, whenever a person working for the Lord causes no stir and makes the Lord's work to have neither sound nor smell, it is needless to inquire—it must be that the life within him is restricted, and the law of life cannot work through.

If you would not misunderstand me, I would testify that many times I dare not spend time in prayer. If I pray only half an hour every day, the wheel of life begins turning, the law of life begins regulating, and the motivating power begins to urge within me, until I cannot bear any longer not to go to work. And even if I have to die there, I have to work. If I do not work, I suffer; but if I work, I am satisfied. Oh, here lies the motivating power of work!

E. It Can Cause Our Service
to Be Living and Fresh

Fifthly, this power can cause us to have living and fresh service. The service of the Old Testament is according to letter. Since it is old, it is dead, and it deadens man. The service of the New Testament is according to the Spirit; it is fresh, and therefore it is living and makes man alive. Old Testament service is an activity based on outward dead rules; therefore, it cannot give man the supply of life. New Testament service is the outcome of the regulating of the law of life in the spirit. It comes from life; therefore, it can give man life and cause him to receive a living supply. Take for example the activities we have in the meetings. If the law of life within us is moving, then even sharing a few words, giving a testimony, or making an announcement can be living, causing man to receive the supply of life.

We become competent ministers of the New Testament with living service, not by our own capability, eloquence or education, but by the Spirit of God (2 Cor. 3:5-6) and according to "the gift of the grace of God" (Eph. 3:7). Such a gift does not refer to the supernatural gifts, such as speaking in tongues, seeing visions, healing, casting out demons, etc., but

to the gift of grace, which is given us according to the working
of the power of God, and which is gained by us because of the
continuous working of the power contained in the life freely
given to us by God. Therefore, the apostle Paul says that this
gift of grace can enable him to preach the unsearchable riches
of Christ and make all men see what is the mystery hidden
throughout the ages in God who created all things (Eph.
3:8-9). Oh, what a great gift this is! Yet such a great gift is
given to him according to the working of the power of the law
of the life of God. Therefore, the gift of grace we receive by the
working of the power of the law of the life of God is fully able
to make us serve God in a living and fresh way.

VIII. THE RESULT OF THE LAW OF LIFE

When we allow the law of the life of God to work unhin-
dered in us in ever-expanding spheres, the life of God within
us can then spread to such a degree that "Christ be formed"
in us (Gal. 4:19). When Christ is thus gradually formed in us,
we are gradually transformed into the image of the Lord
(2 Cor. 3:18) and have the image of the Son of God (Rom. 8:29)
until eventually we are entirely "like him" (1 John 3:2). This
is the glorious result of the working of the law of life within
us.

What does it mean for Christ to be formed in us? We shall
use a simple example. Within an egg, there is the life of a
chicken. Yet in the first few days when the chick is being
formed, if we use an electric light to see through the egg,
we cannot distinguish which part is the head and which
is the feet. When the end of the hatching period approaches,
and the little chick within is just about to break the shell and
come out, if we again use an electric light to see through, we
shall see within the shell the completed form of a chick. This
means that the chick has been formed in the egg. Likewise, when Christ is formed in us, it means that the form
of Christ is completed within us. When we received the life of
Christ through regeneration, Christ was only born in us,
which means He was complete organically, but not complete
in form. Later, as the law of this life works repeatedly in our
inward parts, the element of this life is gradually increased in

our various parts; thus, Christ grows within us until His life is completely formed in us.

As Christ is gradually formed in us, we are also gradually transformed. To the extent that Christ is formed in us, to that extent we are transformed. The formation of Christ and our transformation proceed simultaneously both within and without. As the formation of Christ is the increase of the element of Christ in our various parts from within to without, so our transformation is also in these various parts from within to without, until gradually we become like Christ. Thus, the transformation proceeds from the spirit to the understanding (or the soul), and then to the conduct (or the body). When our spirit is quickened by regeneration, it is transformed by renewal. (See pp. 36-37, concerning the new spirit.) Later, by the working of the law of life, the understanding in the soul is also transformed by renewal. Then, by the shining of the light of the life of God, we recognize our self, we resist our self, and by the Holy Spirit we crucify our self and allow only the life of God to live out from us. Thus, in our spiritual experiences, we put off the old man and put on the new man more and more in our conduct; therefore, our outward conduct is also gradually renewed and transformed. Thus, Christ formed in us means that our nature is being transformed into the likeness of the Lord. When we are being transformed from the spirit through the understanding to the conduct, it means that our likeness is being transformed into the likeness of the Lord. The result of such transformation always causes us to be like the Lord Jesus, or, in other words, like the glorious human nature of the Lord. This is the conformity to the image of His Son mentioned in Romans 8:29. It is like being molded from the mold of the Son of God. Thus, transformation is the process, and to be like the Lord, or to have the same image and nature as the Lord, is the end result of transformation. This is the work "from glory to glory" which the Lord does on us. How much we should praise the Lord!

We also should realize that the goal of transformation is not only to make us like the Lord or to cause us to have the same image and nature as the Lord, but, even more, to make us completely "like Him." This is "the redemption of our body" spoken of in Romans 8:23. When the Lord comes again and appears to us, He will "fashion anew the body of our humiliation, that it may be conformed to the body of his glory, according to the working whereby he is able even to subject all things unto himself" (Phil. 3:21). Thus, He makes us like Him not only in the nature of our spirit and in the form of our soul and of our conduct, but even completely like Him in the body, which shall be glorious and incorruptible and shall never fade away. This is the final outcome of the working of the law of the life of God within us. Oh, how wonderful! How glorious! Therefore, all we who have this hope should purify ourselves even as He is pure (1 John 3:3). We should, by the light of the life of God, know ourselves and all that is outside of God, and we should deal daily with our sin, the world, the flesh and all of the old creation so that we can be pure, without mixture. Then God can soon attain His glorious purpose, and we can soon enjoy the glory with the Lord.

IX. GOD WANTS TO BE GOD IN THE LAW OF LIFE

In Hebrews 8:10, after God said, "I will put my laws into their mind, and on their heart also will I write them," He said, "And I will be to them a God, and they shall be to me a people." This shows us that God puts His law of life within us because He wants to be our God in this law of life, and He wants us to be His people in this law of life. This sets forth the intention of God, or the purpose of God, and it is a very important matter; therefore, we cannot neglect to examine it.

A. God Wants to Be God to Man

Why did God create man? And why did the devil steal man? These matters are not explicitly revealed in the beginning of the Bible. It was not until God declared the ten commandments on Mount Sinai that God's intention in man was clearly revealed. In the first three commandments we see that He wants to be God to man. And it was not until later, when the devil tempted the Lord in the wilderness and wanted the Lord to worship him, that the intention of the devil in stealing man was revealed; that is, he wants to usurp the position of God and wants man to worship him as God.

This shows us clearly that the struggle between the devil and God rests in the matter of who is God to man and who receives the worship of man. But only God is God; only He is worthy to be the God of man and receive the worship of man. In Old Testament times, He lived among the people of Israel as their God. In the New Testament, through incarnation, He lived among men and declared that He is God. Then, through the Holy Spirit, He lives in the church and is God to man in the church. In the future, in the millennium, He will be God to the whole family of Israel; and He will furthermore dwell among men eternally in the new heaven and new earth and be the eternal God to men.

B. God Would Be Father and Then God

God wants not only to be God to man, but even more to be Father to man. He wants not only that man take Him as God, but even more that man have His life. He wants to be Father to man, thereby being God to man in His life. Only when man has His life and becomes His son can man really know that He is God and really allow Him to be God.

In the morning of His resurrection, the Lord Jesus told Mary Magdalene, "I ascend unto my Father and your Father; and my God and your God" (John 20:17). Here the Lord mentioned first the Father and then God. This means that God must be our Father; then He can be our God. And the Lord Jesus in His prayer on His last night also clearly stated that only when we have the eternal life of God can we know Him, the only true God (John 17:3). Therefore, we must experience God as Father in life; then we can know God as God. The more we allow the life of the Father to work in us, the more we worship and serve this glorious God! God is Father to us because He wants to be our God in this life of the Father. This also means that He wants to be our God in the working of His life.

C. God Wants to Be God in the Law of Life

God is our Father because we have His life. Since His life has entered into us, it also brings the law of this life into us. When the law is working, it regulates God Himself out from us. Thus, God intends to be our God in this law of life.

The Mohammedans indeed worship the God in heaven, and even more those in Judaism worship the God in heaven. But they only worship an objective God, a God who is high above all; they have not allowed God to be their God within them. Today, even among Christians, many worship an objective and far-above-all God. They only worship a God outside of them, according to certain outward teachings or rules of letter. They have not allowed God to be a living God to them in the life which is within them. But we must be clear that when we worship God and allow God to be our God, we should not follow the doctrines or laws of letter; rather we should do it in the life of God or in the law of the life of God. This law is the function manifested by the life of God. When this law of the life of God regulates within us, or when God works within us, God is being our God in this law, that is, in His working.

Today when we serve God, we must serve Him in the law of this life, in His working. Whenever we allow His life to work within us and the law of His life to regulate within us, our service is the service of life, spiritual service, or living service. When we thus allow God to be our God in the law of His life, then the God we worship is not a God in doctrine or imagination, but a living God, a practical God, a God who can be touched. In our experiences of life, in our daily living, and in the activities of our work, our God is indeed a living God, a God whom we can touch and whom we can meet. He is not our God in belief; neither is He our God in rules; but He is our God in a living law of life, in a living function of life.

But sometimes, due to some problem in our heart, we do not love Him nor allow the law of His life to regulate us. Then, though we have God, yet God becomes a God in doctrine or in belief. When we recover our former love toward Him and again allow Him to regulate within us by the revolving wheel of His life, then the function of the wheel of His life is again manifested, and the law of His life again does its work of continually moving and regulating within us. At this time, He again becomes our God in a practical sense; He is no longer a name nor a doctrine, but a living God.

Hence we must put ourselves in the hand of God, letting the law of the life of God regulate us; then we can actually have God as our God. Whenever we do not allow this law of life to regulate us, God cannot be our God, and we cannot be His people. For Him to be our God and for us to be His people in a very practical way, we must allow the law of His life to regulate us and allow Him to be our God in the law of His life.

God must be our God in the law of His life, and we must be His people in the law of His life, because our relationship with God must be living. When His life moves and regulates within us, His law of life brings Him to us and brings us to Him. It is in the working of His law of life that we can obtain Him and He can obtain us. Whenever His law of life within us ceases to regulate, this living relationship of Him as our God and us as His people also ceases. Therefore, we must allow the law of the life of God to regulate us; only then can we have God as our God and we be His people in a manifestly living way.

Thus, we can see clearly that God being God to man in the Old Testament and in the New Testament differ very greatly. In the Old Testament, God was God to the people of Israel high above all on His throne, and according to the regulations of law. He also wanted the people of Israel to be His people according to these regulations. Therefore, if they only followed these regulations, they had no problem before God. But in the New Testament, God enters into us to be our life, and it is in the law of this life that He is our God and we are His people. Therefore, it is necessary that we live by the law of this life.

X. CONCLUSION

By seeing the main points of every aspect of the law of life, we know how important this law of life is to our experience of spiritual life. Therefore, we must see clearly and understand thoroughly every main point concerning this subject; then we can have real experience in life. Hence, without fear of repetition, we shall again summarize these main points so that we may have a deep impression of them.

When we become regenerated, we receive the life of God. At this time, though we have the life of God in us, this life is only complete organically; it does not have the completion of growth and maturity. For this we must allow the power of this life to work within us continually and unceasingly in order to reach His perfect goal of growth and maturity. The working of this life comes from the natural function and characteristic of this life; in other words, it comes from the law of this life.

If this law of life is to regulate its contents out of us, it must pass through our heart; therefore, the working of this law of life within us requires the cooperation of our heart. As soon as our heart cooperates, this law of life has an opportunity to regulate within us freely. The result is that it causes us to have a certain consciousness within. When we have this consciousness, we must obey it by the power of this life. Whenever we obey, we let this law have another opportunity to regulate us, thus giving us another consciousness and causing us to proceed further in obedience. The more we obey, the more we afford Him the opportunity to work. Such continued interaction of cause and effect working within us results in the unceasing manifestation of the functions of the two elements, death and resurrection, contained in life. The function of death takes away all that we should not have within us. The function of resurrection adds in all that is of the life of God. Furthermore, the working of this law and these two functions of death and resurrection are also full of power to enable us to answer the unlimited demand of God and live out all that is in the life of God. Thus, we allow the life of God to grow up gradually and mature within us.

In the meantime, when this life works within us, constantly regulating us, our inclination toward God, submission to God, and service to God become natural and easy, living and fresh. It is in this living law that God becomes our living God and we become His living people. We may say that our relationship with God is all in this law of life. This really deserves our deep attention!

Chapter Eleven

THE INWARD KNOWLEDGE

We shall now see the eleventh main point concerning life, which is the inward knowledge, or the knowing of God by the inward law of life and the teaching of the anointing. The degree to which we know God from within determines how much we have of God and how much we experience Him as our life. Thus, the inward knowledge and the growth of life are fully related. If we want to know life so that life may grow, we must examine in detail the inward knowledge.

I. THE IMPORTANCE OF KNOWING GOD

God delights in man knowing Him; therefore, He wants man to "follow on to know" Him (Hosea 6:6, 3). All that He does in the New Testament is in order that we may know Him (Heb. 8:10-11). When we are regenerated, His Spirit, containing His life, enters into us that we may have the capability of knowing Him from within. This knowing of Him, on the one hand, gradually increases with our inward growth of life, and, on the other hand, it also causes the life within us to grow. Because God has given us His life, we can know Him. The more His life grows within us, the more we know Him. The more we know Him, the more we will experience Him as our life, enjoy Him, and allow Him to live out through us. Thus, we may say that all the growth of our spiritual life depends on our knowledge of God. Let us pray that God may give us a spirit of wisdom and revelation so that we may really know Him (Eph. 1:17) and be "growing by the full knowledge of God" (Col. 1:10).

II. THE THREE STEPS OF KNOWING GOD

Psalm 103:7 says: "He made known his ways unto Moses,

his doings unto the children of Israel." This tells us that the children of Israel knew God's doings, but that Moses knew His ways. Hebrews 8:10-11 says also: "I will put my laws into their mind...all shall know me, from the least to the greatest of them." By this verse we see that all who receive the inward law under the New Testament can know God Himself. These two passages in the Bible show us that man's knowledge of God is obtained in three steps: firstly, knowing the doings of God; secondly, knowing the ways of God; and thirdly, knowing God Himself.

A. Knowing the Doings of God

Man knows the doings of God by what He does and performs. For example, the children of Israel in Egypt saw the ten plagues that God sent to smite the Egyptians. By the Red Sea, they saw that God divided the water so they could pass through. In the wilderness, they saw that God commanded the rock to flow out with water to satisfy their thirst. And daily God sent manna from heaven to feed them. When they witnessed such miracles of God, they knew the doings of God. Again, for example, when the multitudes saw the miracles the Lord Jesus performed, such as feeding five thousand people with five loaves and two fishes, calming the storm and the sea, healing the diseased, casting out demons, and raising the dead, they knew His doings. Or, for example, when we are sick and are healed by God, when we meet danger and are preserved by God, when we have needs and are supplied by God, we are made to know the doings of God. When we thus know the doings of God, this is our first step in knowing God. Such knowledge is shallow and outward, for it is not until we see the doings of God that we know what God has done.

B. Knowing the Ways of God

To know God's ways refers to knowing the principles by which He does things. When Abraham pleaded for Sodom, he recognized that God is righteous, and that He will never act contrary to His righteousness. Therefore, Abraham spoke to God according to the righteousness of God (Gen. 18:23-32). This means that he knew the ways by which God does things.

When the children of Israel continued to murmur after Korah and his band rebelled and were consumed, Moses, having seen the appearing of the glory of Jehovah, said unto Aaron: "Take thy censer, and put fire therein from off the altar, and lay incense thereon, and carry it quickly unto the congregation, and make atonement for them: for there is wrath gone out from Jehovah; the plague is begun" (Num. 16:46). This shows that Moses knew the ways of God. He knew that when man acts in a certain way, God will react accordingly.

Samuel told Saul: "Behold, to obey is better than sacrifice, and to hearken than the fat of rams" (1 Sam. 15:22). And David said, "Neither will I offer burnt-offerings unto Jehovah my God which cost me nothing" (2 Sam. 24:24). This shows that they knew the ways of God.

When we release the word of the Lord, we deeply believe that it shall not be void, but shall accomplish that which the Lord pleases (Isa. 55:10-11). Also, if we sow unto the Spirit, we know that we shall of the Spirit reap eternal life (Gal. 6:8). This is also because we know the ways of God.

When we know the ways by which God does things, we have the second step of knowing God. Such knowledge is one step further than knowing the doings of God. Before the doings of God are carried out, we know what He will do and how He will do it. Such knowledge can increase our faith in prayer, and can also enable us to negotiate with God. However, though such knowledge is good, it is still not sufficiently deep and inward.

C. Knowing God Himself

To know God Himself is to know the nature of God. As soon as we are regenerated and receive the life of God, we have the nature of God. Through the life of God within us, we can touch the nature of God. When we touch the nature of God, we touch God Himself; in other words, we know God Himself. Such knowledge is different from the first two steps of knowing God's doing and His ways from without. This is knowing God Himself from within.

For example, consider a brother who had an incurable sickness, but who was actually healed by God. He exclaims happily: "Thank God, He really cared for me!" From this, he knew a little about the doings of God. Later he was sick again. This time he knew it was because he had some fault and God was chastening and disciplining him. Thus, he dealt with his fault. When he had done this, he knew God would heal him (1 Cor. 11:30-32). The result was that God did actually heal him. But before he was healed, he already knew God would heal him. This was because he knew the ways of God. At this time, though his knowledge of God had improved—from knowing God's doings to knowing His ways—yet still it was an objective knowledge of God from without, not a subjective knowledge of God from within. Later, this brother felt from within that he had certain things which were not in accord with the holy nature of God; so he dealt with them and eliminated them. Such feeling and such knowing did not come from anything outside of him, but from the consciousness given to him by the inward life of God. Hence, this time he came to know God Himself from within; he had a subjective knowledge of God.

Consider another brother who in the beginning of a severe difficulty prayed to God, and God carried him through. He thus knew the doings of God. Later, when he again met a difficulty, he knew how he should act so that he could be carried through by God. This indicates that he knew the ways of God. Finally, when he again met a difficulty, he had strangely within him a sense. He sensed that God would definitely carry him through. This sense or knowing was not due to his seeing certain doings of God from without, or from knowing the principles by which God does things. It was because he had touched God Himself from within; therefore, he had this sense or this knowing. Such knowledge of God can be said to be the highest, the deepest, and the most inward.

In Old Testament times, God manifested only His doings and His ways to men. Therefore, at that time man could only obtain the first two steps of knowing God. Now that the New Testament time has come, though we still should know the doings and the ways of God, yet the most important and glorious thing is that God Himself in the Spirit dwells within us to become our life. This enables us to directly touch God Himself and to know Him from within. This third step of knowing God, the knowing of God Himself, is a special blessing to us who are saved under the new covenant.

III. THE TWO KINDS OF KNOWLEDGE OF GOD

Though our knowledge of God is in three steps, there are actually only two kinds of knowledge: the outward knowledge and the inward knowledge. To know the doings and the ways of God are both knowledge of an outward nature. Though these two steps of knowledge differ in degree of depth, yet they are both a knowledge of God derived from the doings and the ways of God outside of us. Therefore, they are objective and outward. Yet to know God Himself is knowledge of an inward kind. This kind of knowledge comes as we touch God Himself by His life within and thereby know Him in a subjective and inward way.

In the original text of the Bible, there are two different words used to describe the inward and outward knowledge. Hebrews 8:11 speaks of our knowing the Lord. The word "know" is used twice in this verse, yet in the original text, two different words were used with different meanings. The first "know" refers to our general, outward knowledge, for which we need the teaching of men. The second "know" refers to the knowledge of our inward sense, for which we do not need man's teaching. This indicates that the outward and inward knowledge of God are indeed different.

For example, suppose we put some fine, white sugar side by side with some fine, white salt. In outward appearance, both are white and fine, and it is difficult to distinguish between them. We may ask someone to tell us which is sugar and which is salt, but this knowledge comes from the teaching of others and is outward, objective, and general. It can also be mistaken. Yet if we simply taste them, we immediately can taste which is sweet and therefore, is sugar, and which is salty and therefore is salt. We do not need others to tell us. This knowing is derived from the sense within; so it is subjective and belongs to the inner sense.

Whenever we taste God from within, we have an enjoyment and taste that cannot be obtained by the knowledge of

God according to His doings or ways from without. Psalm 34:8 says: "Oh taste and see that the Lord is good." Thank God, He can be tasted! Hebrews 6:4-5 says also: "Those who were once enlightened and tasted of the heavenly gift, and were made partakers of the Holy Spirit, and tasted the good word of God, and the powers of the age to come." This shows us that not only can God be tasted, but the things of God, the things of the Spirit, can also be tasted. This tasting causes us to know from within. Once we "taste" God and the things of God from within, we naturally have a certain, accurate knowledge which comes from the inner sense, and we do not need others to teach us. This is indeed a glorious blessing under the new covenant!

IV. THE INWARD KNOWLEDGE

In the New Testament, there are four places which speak very clearly of the inward knowledge. The first two are in Hebrews 8:11 and 1 John 2:27. Both of these say that we do not need others to teach us, but that we can know God from within. However, they say it differently. Hebrews 8 says that the law of the life of God, which is the natural function of the life of God, can cause us to know God. And 1 John 2 says that the teaching of the anointing, which is the revealing moving of the Holy Spirit, can cause us to know God. To know God by the law of life is to know Him by His life. To know God by the teaching of the anointing is to know Him by His Spirit.

The other two places which speak of the inward knowledge are John 17:3 and Ephesians 1:17. John 17:3 says that those who have the eternal life of God are those who know God. This means that God's life within can cause us to know Him. Ephesians 1:17 says that God gives us the spirit of wisdom and revelation so that we may know Him. The spirit mentioned here is our human spirit related to the Spirit of God. This means that our spirit with the Spirit of God can cause us to know God from within.

These four passages in the Bible show us that our inward knowledge of God is by two means: one is by the law of life, which comes from the life of God; the other is by the teaching of the anointing, which comes from the Holy Spirit of God.

Because we have these two means of knowing God within us, our knowledge of God can be in two phases. The law of life primarily causes us to know the nature of God, which is the characteristic of His life. Whenever His life works and functions in us to express this characteristic, it naturally manifests the nature of God to us and causes us to know it. The teaching of the anointing primarily makes us know God Himself. This is because the teaching of the anointing comes from the Holy Spirit, and the Holy Spirit is the embodiment of God Himself. When the Holy Spirit anoints and works in us, He always anoints God Himself into us, thus causing us to know God Himself. The law of life and the teaching of the anointing cause us to know from within the nature of God and God Himself. This is what we call here the inward knowledge.

V. THE LAW AND THE PROPHETS

We can see a shadow of these two phases of the knowledge of the nature of God and God Himself in the Old Testament. God gave the law and the prophets in order that the children of Israel might know His nature and Himself through them. This knowledge was from without.

The characteristics of the Old Testament are the law and the prophets. The reason God gave the law and established the prophets was to cause His people to know Him. Thus, the law and the prophets are the two means by which God led the people of Israel to know Him. By these two means, they could have the knowledge of God in two phases.

God gave the law in order to lead the Israelites to know His nature. The law comes from the nature of God, for it speaks of what God likes and dislikes. Everything the nature of God likes is what He wanted them to do. Everything that the nature of God detests is what He forbade them to do. For example: God is a jealous God; therefore, He forbade them to worship idols. God is loving; therefore, He forbade them to kill. God is holy; therefore, He wanted them to be holy. God is honest; therefore, He wanted them to be honest. The type of law that was given to them was according to the type of nature God has. Thus, the whole law showed the nature of

God to them. Some items speak of the brightness of God, others of the holiness and goodness of God, and still others of the love of God. God used the demanding and forbidding of every item of the law to lead the people of Israel to know every aspect of His nature.

God also established prophets in order to lead the people of Israel to know Himself; for the prophets of the Old Testament were established by God to represent Himself, His Person. The words they spoke were the revelation and guidance given by God according to His own will. For example, Moses was a prophet established by God (Deut. 18:15). The words he spoke to the children of Israel concerning the building of the tabernacle were the revelation of God to them concerning that matter. When he led them to walk in the wilderness, it was God who led them to walk in the wilderness. Thus, God used all kinds of revelation and guidance by the prophets to lead the children of Israel to know Him, His Person.

Since the law is derived from the nature of God, its character is fixed and unchangeable. The law says that one should honor his parents, should not kill, should not commit adultery, and should not steal. These are all fixed, ironclad laws and cannot be changed. They are just as applicable to one person as to another, or to one living in Jerusalem as to one in Samaria. They are not altered due to the change of person, event, time, or place. If the children of Israel were willing to accept the standard of these laws, not only would they know the eternal and unchangeable nature of God, but the style, character, and taste of their living would also correspond to that nature.

On the other hand, since the prophets represented God Himself and spoke out the will of God for a particular time, their activity was flexible and could be changed. It was not limited and fixed. This is because God does all things according to His own will, and He Himself is flexible and cannot be limited. The prophets may at one time give people one kind of revelation, and at another time give another kind of revelation. Here they may give people this kind of guidance, and there they may give them that kind of guidance. Thus, the standard of the law given to men was fixed and limited. But the revelation and guidance which the prophets gave to them was flexible and unlimited. If the Israelites were willing to follow the revelation and guidance of the prophets, they could know God in His very Person by them, and they could know His will for that time. They could also make themselves correspond to God Himself and to His will, whether in action or in rest, in work or in battle.

VI. THE LAW OF LIFE
AND THE TEACHING OF THE ANOINTING

Though the law and the prophets of the Old Testament could cause the children of Israel to know God, it was all outward knowledge, not inward. Therefore, in New Testament times, God put His Spirit with His life in us, thus enabling us to have an inward knowledge of Him. The law of life, which comes from His life, takes the place of the law of the Old Testament and enables us to know His nature from within. The teaching of the anointing takes the place of the prophets of the Old Testament, and enables us to know God Himself and His will from within.

A. The Law of Life

The law of life is a natural characteristic and function of life, and this characteristic of life is the nature of life. Therefore, when the law of the life of God in us expresses its function and regulates us, it always reveals to us the nature of God. It therefore enables us to know the nature of God. Such knowing does not require the teaching of outward knowledge, neither does it need the outward regulations of the law of letters and ordinances, but is by the natural consciousness given to us by the inward law of life. For example, if vinegar is put in the mouth of a baby, he will spit it out. But if sugar is put in his mouth, he will swallow it. The baby's ability to distinguish between the sour and sweet is not based upon teaching, but upon the natural function of life. Likewise, one who is just saved and has received the life of God does not like to commit sin. It is not because he is afraid of the punishment of sin, but because the holy nature of the life of God within him naturally gives him a loathsome, detestable, and unbearable consciousness toward sin. Such consciousness is deeper than the condemnation of the conscience. It is from such a consciousness of detesting sin that we come to know the holy nature of God.

Paul told the saints in Corinth that "we toil, working with our own hands: being reviled, we bless; being persecuted, we endure; being defamed, we entreat" (1 Cor. 4:12-13). Paul could behave in this way not only because the life of God in him made him this way, but also because the nature of the life of God in him is this way. When he lived in the life of God in that manner, he then touched the nature of God; in other words, he came to know the nature of God.

The nature of the life of God, such as holiness, love, honesty, brightness, etc., is always unchangeable from eternity to eternity, regardless of difference of time or place. Therefore, the character of the law of His life is also fixed and unchangeable. Regardless of time or place, whenever the law of the life of God works, the nature of God which it enables us to touch is always permanent and unchangeable.

When the law of life is working in us, enabling us to know the nature of God, the result is that it makes the manner, character, and taste of our entire living correspond to the nature of God. It is not like the law of letters of the Old Testament, which is only an outward regulation, demanding that the outward life of man correspond with the nature of God. This is the law of life of the New Testament, which, by the working of this life within, mingles the nature of God into our nature. Thus, it causes our nature to contain the element of God's nature and gradually become like God's nature. Whatever the nature of God loves or detests, our nature will likewise love or detest. Now, whenever we do or even want to do the dark and unclean things of the past, the law of life within causes us to feel uncomfortable, unnatural, and without peace. Conversely, the more we do the things which are bright and holy and correspond to the nature of God, the more we feel life and peace from within. In this way, our living is naturally changed to correspond with the nature of God from within.

B. The Teaching of the Anointing

In the Scriptures, only 1 John 2:27 speaks of the "teaching of the anointing." We all know that anointing is a verbal noun which refers to the activity of the ointment, the moving and the working of the ointment. According to the type of the Old Testament and the fulfillment of the New Testament, ointment or oil in the Scripture refers to the Holy Spirit (Isa. 61:1; Luke 4:18). Since ointment or oil refers to the Holy Spirit, the "anointing" must refer to the working of the Holy Spirit. The working of the Holy Spirit in us is like the anointing of the ointment; therefore, the Scripture calls this working of the Holy Spirit the "anointing."

Since the anointing is the Holy Spirit's working in us, it naturally causes us to have an inner sense so that we may know God and His will. When the anointing causes us to know God and the will of God in this way, it is teaching us from within. Thus, the Scripture calls this teaching, "the teaching of the anointing."

Since the anointing is the working of the Holy Spirit in us, it is also God Himself working in us, because the Holy Spirit is the embodiment of God within us. God is unlimited; therefore, the character of the teaching He gives us from working and anointing within us cannot be limited. Sometimes He gives us this kind of teaching; sometimes He gives us that kind of teaching. It is not like the law of His life, whose character is fixed and unchangeable. The law of His life is from the fixed nature of His life, and it causes us to touch the fixed nature of His life; therefore, the function of this law within us is fixed. But the working of His Holy Spirit is from His unlimited self, and it causes us to touch His unlimited self; therefore, the teaching that this working gives us from within is also unlimited. It can cause us to obtain His revelation and receive His guidance, thereby causing us to know His infinite self and His unlimited will.

Since the teaching of the anointing gives us revelation and guidance by God's infinite self, it can therefore cause all our behavior, action, movement, and choice to be in accord with the will of God. This is not like the prophets of the Old Testament time who taught others from without and demanded that their action should correspond with the will of God. This is the Holy Spirit as the ointment in us, anointing into us the element of God Himself and enabling us from within to comprehend the will of God because of having touched God Himself. The result is that it causes not only our action but our whole being to be filled with the element of God and to be in accord with His will.

Thus, the law of life causes us to touch the nature of the life of God. It regulates from within us according to the nature of the life of God. But the anointing causes us to touch God, to touch His Person, and anoints into us His very essence. Since we have the law of life and the anointing continuously working and teaching in us, we can know God in all things and need not that others should teach us. Whenever we touch the question of the manner and taste of living, the law of life makes known to us the nature of God in these matters. And whenever we touch the question of action or choice, the teaching of the anointing causes us to understand how God Himself feels toward these matters.

For example, suppose we want to purchase some clothes. Whether we buy them or not is a question of being guided by the Holy Spirit in action. Thus, the anointing will teach and guide us. When we get to the store, the style and color we select are matters related to the taste of the nature of God. The law of life will cause us to feel what style and color are in accordance with the nature of God. The guidance of whether we should go to the store and buy the clothes or not is not a fixed one. It is possible that this time we should go, and the next time we should not. Yet the taste of what style and color we should choose is never changed; each time we go, it is the same.

Consider, for example, a brother and sister who want to get married. Which day they should be married is a question of being guided in action; it is not related to the nature of God. It is not that the first day or the fifteenth day would be in accordance with the nature of God, and all other days would not. Since this is a matter of guidance in action, it is determined by the anointing or the working of the Holy

Spirit. Yet at the time of marriage, the style of clothes, the type of setting, how the meeting is arranged, and whether the character, the taste, and the style are in accordance with the church and becoming to the saints, are all matters related to the nature of God. Therefore, they are not taught by the anointing but are regulated by the law of life.

C. The Connection between These Two

Though the law of life and the teaching of the anointing have different functions and are not the same, yet they are very closely related. The mutual cause and effect of one on the other cannot be separated.

The law of life originates from the life of God, and the life of God rests upon, and is contained in, the Spirit of God. Therefore, this law is also called "the law of the Spirit of life" (Rom. 8:2), and is also a law of the Holy Spirit. Though this law is derived from the life of God and rests with that life, yet it is executed by the Holy Spirit of God, and this working of the Holy Spirit is the anointing. Therefore, the function of this law is necessarily manifested with the anointing. Whenever the anointing stops, the function of this law necessarily disappears. This proves to us that the anointing and the function of the law of life are actually connected together and cannot be separated.

Furthermore, the teaching of the anointing is also related to our comprehension of the law of life. Since the law of life is the natural function of life, the working of this law within us belongs to the sense of life. By the law of this life, we can only have a sense in the deepest part of our being, a sense which makes us feel an urging or forbidding, a liking or a detesting. Yet we still cannot comprehend the meaning of that sense. To understand the meaning of that inner sense, we need the teaching of the anointing. It is only when the anointing teaches us that we can comprehend the meaning of the sense given to us by the law of life. For example, a child who tastes sugar and salt for the first time can by the natural capability of the life within him sense the difference in taste; yet he still does not know what these two things are. However, when his mother tells him that the sweet one is called sugar and the salty one is called salt, he not only senses that the taste of these two things differ, but he also knows what these two things are.

Likewise, when a brother is saved, he has within him the life of God. Therefore, if he goes to the movies, drinks wine or smokes, because all of these things are not in harmony with the nature of the life of God in him, the nature of this life causes him to feel uneasy and to have no peace until he abandons these things. This is what the innate sense of the life of God makes known to him. Yet, though he feels uneasy in doing these things, still he does not understand why he feels uneasy. It is not until the anointing, through the teaching of the Scripture, makes known to him that all of these things are not in accord with the nature of the holy life of God in him that he knows the cause of this uneasiness. At this time, not only does he have the consciousness that the innate sense of the life of God gives him, but he also has the teaching of the anointing which causes him to understand. Thus, not only is the function of the law of life manifested by the anointing, but also the meaning of the sense of the law of life is revealed through the teaching of the anointing.

On the other hand, the working of the law of life is also related to our comprehension of the teaching of the anointing. From experience we know that understanding the teaching of the anointing rests with the growth of life. The extent of our growth of life determines how much we understand the teaching of the anointing. For example, if the child who tasted sugar and salt is too young, even if his mother tells him that the sweet thing is called sugar and the salty thing is called salt, he still cannot comprehend. It is necessary to wait until his life grows to a certain level; then he can comprehend. If we want to comprehend the teaching of the anointing, the same principle applies. The growth of life must be sufficient. If we want to comprehend more of the teaching of the anointing, our growth of life must increase more. And the increase of the growth of life is from the working of the law of life. The more the law of life works in us, the more our growth of life will increase, and the more we can comprehend the teaching of the anointing. Thus, the working of the law of life can increase our comprehension of the anointing.

Therefore, let us remember that the law of life and the anointing not only are related to one another, but also influence one another. It is the relatedness and interaction of these two which make our inward knowledge of God grow more and more until we fully and richly know God.

D. The Comparison of These Two

We have already seen how the law of life and the teaching of the anointing differ, and how they are mutually and reciprocally related. Now we shall see a simple and clear comparison of the knowledge of God given by these two, which will make us even more clear.

Because the law of life is the natural function of the life of God, the knowledge of God that it gives us is only of one kind; that is, it causes us to know the nature of the life of God.

However, since the teaching of the anointing is the working of the Spirit of God Himself, the knowledge of God that it gives us is at least of three kinds:

First, it causes us to know God Himself. This means that we touch God Himself and thereby experience and gain Him.

Second, it causes us to know the will of God. This means that we understand the guidance that God gives us in our actions. This can be divided into usual guidance and special guidance. Usual guidance is for our daily life. Special guidance is for the plan of the Lord's work. As we have said before, whether we should or should not buy certain clothing, what day we should have a wedding, etc., are all examples of usual guidance in our daily life. On the other hand, when Brother Hudson Taylor felt that he should take the Gospel of the Lord into the interior of China, this was special guidance in the work of the Lord.

Third, it causes us to know truth. This means that we receive revelation concerning truth. This also is divided into the usual and the special. The usual is concerned with our human behavior: for instance, seeing that the believers should not be "unequally yoked together with unbelievers" (2 Cor. 6:14), or that whatsoever we do, we should "do all to the glory of God" (1 Cor. 10:31). On the other hand, special revelation is concerned with the plan of God, such as seeing the mystery of God in Christ (Col. 2:2), and the function of the Church in relation to Christ (Eph. 1:23).

After seeing these points, we realize that the inner knowledge afforded to us by the law of life and the teaching of the anointing is indeed rich. It includes almost all the working of God within us, and thus enables us to have a full, rich, and thorough knowledge of God.

VII. THE PROOF OF THE SCRIPTURE

The inner sense given to us by the law of life and the teaching of the anointing enables us to know God. Yet, even though this inner sense may be absolutely real and true, still it needs to be proved by the teaching and the principles of the Scripture. If the consciousness we have within is not in accord with the teaching and principles of the Scripture, we should not accept it. In this way we can guard against being deceived or going to an extreme, and we can be accurate and stable.

Whether the inner consciousness is from the law of life in our spirit or from the Holy Spirit as the anointing, it should be in accordance with the truth of the Scripture. If the consciousness we feel within us is not in accordance with the truth of the Scripture, then it must not be from the law of life or the teaching of the anointing. Though the consciousness within may be living, yet the truth in the Scripture is accurate and secure. Though the truth of the Scripture alone is only accurate and secure without being living, yet the inner sense alone can sometimes be living but not accurate; or living, but not secure. It is like a train going forward: there should not only be the power inside, but also the tracks outside. Of course, if there are only tracks outside and no power within, the train cannot move. But if there is only power inside and no tracks outside, though the train may move, it definitely will rush into calamity. Therefore, we not only need the living sense within, but also the accurate truth without. The living consciousness within is from the law of life and the teaching of the anointing; the accurate truth without rests in the teaching of the written words of the Scripture and the light of its principles.

When the children of Israel walked in the wilderness, a pillar of cloud was their guide during the day, and a pillar of fire their leading at night. Likewise, when our spiritual condition is as the broad daylight, when we are inwardly as bright as noon and our inner sense is clear and accurate, with the guidance of the Holy Spirit as typified by the pillar of cloud, then we can walk in the right path of God. But at times, our spiritual condition is like the dimness of night; within we are as dark as midnight, and our inner sense is blurred and unclear. Then we need the Scripture, typified by the pillar of fire, to be the lamp to our feet and the light for our path to lead us to walk in the upright way of God.

Therefore, if we desire to walk in the safe way of life and truth, we should check and prove every consciousness, guidance, and revelation by the teaching and principles of real power and secure strength. Only this balance will enable us to go forward without being one-sided.

VIII. THE OUTWARD "TEACHING"

Though on the one hand the Scripture says that, because we have the law of life and the teaching of the anointing within us, we can know God and do not need others to teach us, yet on the other hand there are many places in Scripture which speak of the teaching of man. For instance, such passages as 1 Corinthians 4:17; 14:19; 1 Timothy 2:7; 3:2; 2 Timothy 2:2, 24, etc., say that the apostle Paul taught men, and he wanted others also to learn how to teach men. There are three main reasons for this.

First, although the inner sense given to us by the law of life and the teaching of the anointing is sufficient to make us know God, and thus we do not need the teaching of men, yet we often do not listen and do not heed such consciousness. We are weak, especially in hearing God's words. Sometimes we do not hear, and sometimes we are not willing to hear. Those who are sick in their minds, those who are subjective, those who insist on their own opinions, and those who intentionally close themselves often cannot hear. And those who do not love the Lord, who will not pay the price and who will not follow the Lord, are not willing to hear. Because they are not willing to hear, they naturally do not hear. Because they do not hear, they even more would not hear. Therefore, many times it is not that God does not speak, that His life does not regulate, or that His anointing does not teach, but that we do not hear. Job 33:14 says: "God speaketh once, yea twice, though man regardeth it not." We have conditions worse than this. Even when God speaks five, ten or twenty times, we still would not listen. But, thank God, He is forgiving and longsuffering. If we do not listen to what He says within, He uses the teaching of men from without to repeat. He has already spoken within us, but because we do not hear, He teaches us from without through men to repeat what He has already said within.

Under the New Testament, much teaching follows this principle of repeating. In the Epistles, this saying, "Know ye not?" occurs frequently. This is to say that you have already heard and known, but you do not mind and hear; therefore, God uses men to teach you again. Thus, many times, whether God uses the words of the Scripture or His servant to teach us, He does not do it to replace His teaching within us, but to repeat what He has already taught us within. Though the outward guidance and the inward teaching are of mutual help to each other, yet the outward cannot take the place of the inward. It is only a repetition of the inward.

Thus, today when we help others in spiritual matters, we should not give them the ten commandments in order to teach them to act in this way or in that in an objective way. We can only explain what God has ordained in principle, thus bearing witness to the words that God speaks from within and repeating what God has already taught them from within. We should not objectively teach men in this way or in that way in detail. This is what the prophets of the Old Testament did. In the New Testament, there are only the prophets for the church, explaining what God has ordained in principle. There is no prophet for individuals, deciding on matters in detail. The settlement of details is what God, by the law of life and the teaching of the anointing, makes known to every man

from within. This is the principle of the New Testament.
Thus, though we should be humble to receive teaching from
others, yet it must be what the law of life within us has regulated or the anointing has already taught that governs us.
Otherwise, it will not be in accord with the New Testament
principle.

The second reason for the teaching of man in the New
Testament is that, though the law of life and the anointing
can cause us to know God, yet the consciousness and teaching
they give to us are all in our spirit. If we do not receive
adequate teaching from without, it is difficult for our mind to
comprehend the consciousness and teaching given in our
spirit by the law of life and the anointing. In order for our
mind to comprehend the consciousness and teaching given
to us by the law of life and the anointing from within, we need
men to teach us the way of God from without. The more we
receive such outward teaching, the more our mind comprehends the consciousness and teaching from the law of
life and the anointing within. And the more we receive such
outward teaching, the more it will help our spirit to grow,
thereby giving the law of life and the anointing even more
ground and opportunity to manifest their functions and give
us a deeper sense and teaching. Therefore, though the law of
life and the anointing do give us consciousness and teaching
from within, we still need the teaching of men from without.
However, this teaching from without cannot and should not
take the place of the consciousness and teaching of the law
of life and the anointing from within. It is only to help us
comprehend this inner sense and teaching and to give opportunity to the law of life and the anointing to give us a deeper
sense and teaching. The teaching of men from without always
should have an "amen" or "echo" from the consciousness and
teaching from within given by the law of life and the anointing. Then it is in accord with the principle of the New
Testament. The teaching and guidance from within and without are not to substitute for each other, but to have a mutual
response.

Third, although the law of life and the teaching of
the anointing can cause us to know God in all things, yet

concerning the truth of the deep things of God and the fundamental knowledge of the spiritual life, we often still need others who have the ministry of words in God's revelation to teach us that we may understand. We need the subjective knowledge which comes from the anointing and the law of life within, yet often without the objective teaching of others, we cannot obtain the subjective knowledge from within. Of course, under the New Testament, the outward, objective teaching cannot take the place of the inward subjective knowledge; but often the inward, subjective knowledge is attained because of the outward, objective teaching.

For the above three reasons, God often raises up those who have spiritual knowledge and experience before God and arranges for them to teach and guide us. Let us hope that on one hand we may reverence what God teaches us from within through the law of life and the anointing, and that on the other hand we would not ignore the teaching God gives to us through men from without. We should not refuse the teaching of men from without simply because we have the law of life and the teaching of the anointing within. We do thank God for giving us the law of life and the teaching of the anointing, but we still should humble and empty ourselves to receive the teaching and guidance God gives to us through men. Let us remember that under the New Testament, God not only gives us the law of life and the anointing to teach us from within, but He also gives those who can teach and guide us from without.

IX. KNOWING IN THE SPIRIT
AND UNDERSTANDING IN THE MIND

A. Knowing in the Spirit

Since the inward knowledge issues from the law of life and from the teaching of God's Spirit as the anointing, and both are in our spirit, this knowledge from within will definitely be made known to us in our spirit. Except for the questions of right and wrong, which are determined by the conscience part of our spirit, this knowing in the spirit can be said to be the responsibility of the intuition part of our spirit. Therefore, if we want to understand the inward knowledge, we must know what the intuition of the spirit is.

Both the body and soul of man have senses. As the body has the sense of sight, hearing, smell, taste, and touch, and the soul has the sense of happiness, anger, sorrow, and joy, etc., so the spirit of man has a sense of the conscience and a sense of the intuition. The sense of the conscience occurs due to questions of right and wrong; the sense of the intuition occurs directly without a cause. Scripture shows us that the spirit can be "willing" (Matt. 26:41), it can "perceive" the reasoning of man's heart (Mark 2:8), it can "sigh deeply" (Mark 8:12), it can purpose (Acts 19:21), and it can be "provoked," "fervent," and "refreshed," etc. (Acts 17:16; 18:25; 2 Cor. 7:13). All of these are the senses of the intuition of the spirit. We may say that the intuition of the spirit has just as many senses as the soul.

Yet the intuition of the spirit differs from the sense of the soul. The main difference is that the sense of the soul springs from a cause, but the intuition of the spirit is without a cause. The cause of the sense of the soul is but from men, events, and outward things. Whether it be a man, an event or a thing, it can cause us to have a soulish consciousness. If it is delightful, we are happy; if it is sorrowful, we feel sorry. Such senses of the soul which are due to outward influences are senses with a cause. Yet the intuition of the spirit is without a cause, which means it is without a means, but is directly present in the deep part of the spirit. Not only is it not influenced by men, events or things from without; it is also not influenced by the sense of the soul. In fact, it often acts contrary to the sense of the soul.

For example, sometimes we want to do a certain thing. Our reasons are quite sufficient, our heart is also very happy, and we have willed to carry it out. Yet we do not know why we have in our spirit an unspeakable condition. We feel very heavy and depressed, as if the spirit is opposing what our mind thinks, our emotion likes, and our will has determined. Our spirit seems to be saying that we should not carry out what we have planned. Such a consciousness is the forbidding of the intuition of the spirit. Sometimes there is a certain matter which has no reason to support it; it is also contrary to our likes, and we are not willing to carry it out. Yet, though we know not why, we constantly feel in the spirit a kind of urging and moving, desiring us to carry it out. Once we do it, we feel comfortable within. Such consciousness is the urging of the intuition in the spirit.

Such forbidding or urging of the intuition in the spirit occurs without a cause. It is a deeper sense which occurs because of the working of the law of life and the anointing. Because of this, we can directly touch God, know God, and know His will. Such knowing in the intuition of the spirit is what the Scripture speaks of as "revelation." Thus, revelation is nothing but the Holy Spirit in our spirit showing us the reality of a particular event so that we may comprehend it clearly. Such knowledge can be said to be the deepest knowledge of God within us. It is also the inward knowledge of which we are speaking.

B. Understanding in the Mind

Although the inward knowledge is in the intuition of our spirit, it still must be understood by the mind of our soul. This is because the organ of understanding and comprehension is the mind. Therefore, the inward knowledge needs not only to be known by the spirit, but also to be comprehended by the mind. The knowing of the intuition in the spirit must have added to it the understanding of the mind in order to have comprehension. The understanding of the mind is a kind of interpretation by the mind of the intuition of the spirit. Whenever we have an intuitive consciousness in our spirit, our mind is needed to understand and interpret it. This means that we take the related men, events or things and check them with this intuitive consciousness of the spirit. We check until the spirit echoes. We then know the intention of the Holy Spirit and can take action accordingly.

For example, when we come to the Lord, and feel a burden in the intuition deep within, we know that guidance from God has come to us. This is a knowing in the spirit. Yet we may not be clear whether this guidance from God is for us to preach the Gospel or to visit a brother. If it is to visit a brother, which brother should we visit? All of this requires the mind to understand. We should, in our mind, place before God one by one all the things that we should do and check with the intuition within. If when we come to the matter of visiting the brothers there is a response within, then we understand God wants us to visit some brothers. Then in this fellowship with God we further bring forward, one by one, many brothers who we should visit and check with the intuition of the spirit. When we check concerning the brother who is in need, there may be no response in the spirit. When we check concerning the brother who is sick, there may also be no response in the spirit. But when we consider another brother who has gotten into trouble, the intuition in the spirit responds, and it is as if the inside of our whole being says, "Amen!" If we are afraid we may be wrong, we may take more of the brothers who need to be visited and check them too. If the spirit does not respond to any of them, we understand that the person God wants us to visit is the brother who has gotten into trouble. This is using the mind to understand what is known in the spirit, or using the mind to interpret the consciousness in the spirit.

Another example is that in prayer you may have a burden, feeling that God wants you to say something to the brothers and sisters. This burden is the knowing in the intuition. Yet as to what God wants you to say, you are not clear. This requires that in your mind you take one message after another and check them with the burden in your spirit. When you check the matter of dealing with the flesh, the spirit responds. Then you understand that God wants you to speak on this subject. This understanding is the comprehension of the mind. Thus, the burden of the intuition in the spirit makes known to you that God wants you to do something, and the understanding of the mind in the soul enables you to comprehend what the thing is that God wants you to do.

Perhaps on the Lord's day, as usual, you want to offer some money. But your spirit has a burden, a feeling that God wants you to give a special offering. But how much God wants you to offer, for what matter, and for which person must be understood in the mind. In this way, not only do you have in the intuition the burden of God, but you also understand in the mind the intention of God. This, then, is the inward knowledge.

Such a way of doing things may seem quite awkward. Yet, when a man is just beginning to learn to interpret the consciousness of the spirit with his mind, he should carry it out in this way. Later, when he has learned to be habitual in so doing and has become proficient, as soon as there is the consciousness or knowing in the spirit, the mind immediately can comprehend and understand.

X. THE WAY OF OBTAINING THE INWARD KNOWLEDGE

Now that we have seen every aspect of the inward knowledge, we must see the way of practice or the way of obtaining the inward knowledge. To obtain the inward knowledge, we must exercise the spirit, renew the understanding, and deal with the heart.

A. Exercising the Spirit

Since the inward knowledge is in the intuition of our spirit, if we want to obtain such knowledge, we must often exercise and use our spirit so that it is lively and strong. It is only when the spirit is lively and strong that the intuition of the spirit is conscious and alert, thus enabling us to know God from within.

In order to exercise the spirit, we first must learn to turn to the spirit. If we constantly live in the outward man, we have no way to know God in the intuition of the spirit. We must learn to put aside the outward, busy doings and entanglements. We should refrain not only from being so busy outwardly, but also from allowing our thinking to run wild. Instead we should pay attention to the move in the spirit, the consciousness deep within. The child Samuel, ministering to the Lord, could hear His voice; Mary, quietly sitting at the Lord's feet, could understand the Lord's words. If we can thus turn to the spirit to be near to God, we can actually touch the consciousness of God in the spirit and thereby know God.

We also need to exercise and use the spirit in our daily living. Whether dealing with people, managing affairs, handling things, or in meetings serving the Lord and ministering the word of God; whether in conversing with others or even in doing business; in all matters we must deny the soul and let the spirit lead. We must not let our mind, emotion or will lead, but in all things first try to touch the consciousness deep in the spirit. That is, we must first try to ask what the Lord who dwells in the spirit has to say. If we continue to exercise in this way, the consciousness in the spirit will definitely be alert, and it will then be an easy matter for the inward knowledge to increase and deepen.

In exercising the spirit, the best practice is prayer, for prayer requires exercising the spirit more than any other activity. We often love idle talking, but we will not pray or praise; therefore, our spirit is often shriveled up. If we could spend an hour or more in prayer daily, not in asking, but in worshipping, fellowshipping and praising, before long our spirit would definitely grow and become strong. The psalmist said that he praised the Lord seven times a day (Psa. 119:164). If those who practice boxing practice one hour every day, after a certain period of time their fists will be very strong. Likewise, if we exercise our spirit every day to pray, our spirit will definitely become strong. When the spirit is strong, the intuition will surely be alert. We can then, with an alert intuition, obtain more knowledge of God.

B. Renewing the Understanding

We have already mentioned that the inward knowledge requires not only the knowing in the spirit, but also the understanding of the mind. Therefore, if we want to obtain this inward knowledge, we need to exercise our spirit and to renew the understanding of our mind. The mind is the organ for understanding things; understanding is its main capability.

Romans 12:2 shows us that only when the mind, which contains the understanding, is renewed and transformed can we "prove what is the good and acceptable and perfect will of God." Colossians 1:9 also shows us that in having "spiritual understanding" we can "be filled with the knowledge of his will." Therefore, renewing the understanding of the mind is a necessity in the matter of knowing God.

Before we were saved, our total being, including our mind, was fallen. Every imagination of the thoughts of our heart was evil (Gen. 6:5), and our thinking and perception were also filled with the savor of the world. Since our mind was in such a state, our understanding became dimmed. Therefore, we were totally unable to comprehend spiritual things. Even less could we understand the will of God. When we were saved, we were renewed by the Holy Spirit (Titus 3:5). This renewing work of the Holy Spirit begins first in our spirit and then expands to our soul to renew the understanding of our mind that we may know the things of the spirit. The more the understanding of our mind is renewed by the Holy Spirit, the more we can comprehend spiritual things and understand the will of God.

Though this renewing of the understanding of the mind is done by the Holy Spirit, we must bear two responsibilities:

First, we must consecrate ourselves. In Romans 12, before the mind is renewed and transformed, we are asked to present our bodies a living sacrifice. This shows that the renewing of the understanding of the mind is based upon our consecration. If we are really willing to consecrate and give ourselves to God, then the Holy Spirit of God can expand His renewing work into our soul and thereby renew the understanding of our mind.

Second, we must accept the dealings of the cross to cast away the old living of the past. Ephesians 4:22-23 shows us that only when we put away the old man of our former manner of life, can our mind, which contains our understanding, be renewed. Before we were saved, our old way of living had already darkened the understanding of our mind. After we were saved, by the death of the Lord on the cross, we put away the old living of the past. This allows the killing of the Lord's cross to abolish, one by one, all the old ways of living. Only then can the understanding of our mind be renewed. Thus, we must accept the dealings of the cross for the understanding of our mind to be renewed. The degree to which we allow the cross to abolish our old living, to the same extent the understanding of our mind can be renewed.

Ephesians 4:23 says: "Be renewed in the spirit of your

mind." We know that the mind is the main part of the soul. Originally, it was not related to the spirit, but now the spirit has become "the spirit of the mind"; therefore, it is connected to the mind. This is because the spirit has expanded and reached the mind of our soul that we may be renewed in this spirit, that is, that our mind may be renewed by being connected to the spirit. Hence, this renewal is expanded from the spirit to the mind.

The work of the Spirit within is from center to circumference, which also means from the inner spirit to the outer soul. The Spirit first renews our spirit, which is the center of our being within. Then, if we consecrate ourselves to Him and accept the dealings of the cross, He will expand from our spirit to the soul, which is the outer circumference. This will renew every part of our soul. This means that when our soul submits to the ruling of the Spirit and becomes united to our spirit, it is renewed. Therefore, the understanding of the mind is also renewed.

After we receive the regeneration of the Holy Spirit in our spirit, if we consecrate ourselves to God and accept the dealings of the Holy Spirit through the cross to put away our old living, the Holy Spirit can then continuously do His expanding work within us, renewing the understanding of our mind in the soul. Only such a renewed understanding can match the intuition in the spirit. Whenever God makes something known to us in the intuition of our spirit, the understanding of the mind can immediately understand. When we have a strong and alert spirit plus a renewed and clear understanding, we can then have a full inward knowledge of the nature of God and of all His guidance and revelation.

C. Dealing with the Heart

The heart is the aggregate of man; therefore, if the heart has problems, all the activities of the spirit and life within us will suffer hindrance and limitation. Even though our spirit is alert and our understanding is renewed, if there are problems with our heart, we still cannot obtain the inward knowledge of God. Therefore, we must also deal with our heart that it may be soft and clean, loving God, wanting God, and obeying God.

In Matthew 11:25, the Lord says that God has hid the spiritual things from the wise and understanding and has revealed them unto babes. The "wise and understanding" are those who are self-right in their heart, self-satisfied and stubborn; therefore, they cannot see the spiritual things of God. "Babes" are those who are humble and soft in their hearts; therefore, they can receive the revelation of God. Thus, our heart must be dealt with until it is humble and soft. It is only when it is rid of its self-satisfaction and stubbornness that we can receive the inward revelation and knowledge of God.

In Matthew 5:8, the Lord says that "the pure in heart shall see God." If our heart is not pure in that we have inclinations and desires other than God, there is within us a veil which hinders us from seeing God clearly. Yet whenever our heart turns to God, the veil is taken away (2 Cor. 3:16). Thus, we must deal with our heart. Our heart must be pure and not "doubleminded" (James 4:8); then we can receive light and revelation in the spirit, comprehend and understand in the mind, and thus know God.

In John 14:21, the Lord says that "he that loveth me...I will manifest myself unto him." Mary of Magdalene, on the morning of resurrection, because of her keen love for the Lord, sought for Him. She received the first manifestation of the Lord to His disciples after resurrection and became the first one who knew the resurrected Christ (John 20). Brother Lawrence said that if one wants to know God, love is the only way. Our heart must love God and seek God; then we can have the manifestation of God and know Him.

In John 7:17, the Lord says: "If any man willeth to do his will, he shall know..." This reveals that our heart must want God and His will; then we can know God and know the will of God.

In Philippians 2:13, the apostle says that it is God who works in us both to will and to work. If our heart does not submit or is not willing to submit to the working of God within us, God cannot work in us; thus, we cannot receive the consciousness which His working would give us in the knowledge of Himself. Hence, our heart must be dealt with until it not only can submit to God, but is also willing to submit to God. Then we can receive the consciousness and knowledge which comes through the working of God within us.

Therefore, we must (1) exercise and use the spirit until it is strong and alert, (2) have our understanding renewed by the Spirit, and (3) deal with our heart until it is soft and pure, loving God, wanting God, and submissive to God; then we can have the inward knowledge of God.

XI. CONCLUSION

Because God delights that man should know Him, He has given man many ways and means so that he may know Him. In Old Testament times, He manifested His doings and declared His ways to men so that they might know Him. But the knowledge man had of Him by those doings and ways was only outward, objective, shallow, and incomplete. Therefore, at the time of the New Testament, though He still uses His doings and ways to make Himself known to us, the most important and glorious thing is that He Himself as the Spirit has entered into us to be our life. This enables us to have an inward, subjective, deep, and full knowledge of Him.

When God is in us as life, He causes us to have a law of divine life within, which regulates us from within continuously, causing us to know the nature of His life. The law of this life, because it is a law, is not a person; it is fixed and unchangeable. It regulates us within unchangeably according to the nature of the life of God. The result is that it causes the manner, nature, and taste of our living to be in accord with the nature of God.

The Spirit of God dwelling in us is as the ointment, anointing and teaching us to know Himself. Since this ointment is God Himself, it is a person, and it is unlimited and flexible. This ointment in us continuously anoints into us the infinite God Himself. The result is that it causes our whole person, behavior, and conduct to be filled with the essence of God and agree with the will of God.

God, as the law of life and the anointing, begins first in

our spirit and expands then to our soul that our mind might comprehend and understand. Therefore, we need to exercise the spirit that the intuition of the spirit might be alert. We also need to have our mind renewed so that the understanding of our mind can be clear. In addition, we need to deal with our heart that it might be soft and pure, loving God, wanting God, and submissive to God. In this way, as soon as the law of life and the anointing move within us, the intuition in our spirit will immediately know, the understanding of our mind will also immediately comprehend, and we can have the inward knowledge of God at any time.

For such an inward knowledge, God has also given us the teaching and principles of the Bible from without to check and prove us that we may not be mistaken or deceived. In addition, through His many servants from without, God teaches or repeats the consciousnesses we feel from within. He may teach our mind to comprehend the consciousness we have in the spirit, or He may make clear to us the deep things of God and the fundamental knowledge of the spiritual life.

Since from within and without we have so many ways and means to know God, we can "be filled with the knowledge of his will in all spiritual wisdom and understanding, to walk worthily of the Lord unto all pleasing, bearing fruit in every good work, and increasing in the knowledge of God" (Col. 1:9-10). When we know God in this way, we not only can fully know the will of God, but we can also grow and mature in the life of God. The more we increase in the knowledge of God, the more we will grow in the life of God until He completely occupies us. Then the essence of God will be fully wrought into us, thus fulfilling that glorious goal of God's desire to be mingled with us as one.

Chapter Twelve

WHAT IS THE GROWTH OF LIFE?

Now we shall see the twelfth main point concerning the knowledge of life, which is the growth of life. If we desire to have further knowledge of life, we must also know what the growth of life is. There are many brothers and sisters whose hearts' love toward the Lord cannot be said to lack fervency, and the price they have paid also cannot be considered insufficient, yet because they do not know what the real growth of life is, they have many mistaken views and pursuits; thus, the real growth of life in them is quite limited. How unfortunate this is! Therefore, in order that we may have accurate knowledge and proper pursuit in the path of life, we shall spend a little time to see what the growth of life is.

Before we see what the growth of life is, however, we shall look at the negative side, what the growth of life is not. This will make us more deeply impressed and afford a more precise knowledge.

I. GROWTH OF LIFE IS NOT THE IMPROVEMENT OF BEHAVIOR

The improvement of behavior means the changing of a person's behavior from bad to good, from evil to virtuous. This is what men ordinarily call "forsaking evil ways and returning to the right" or "departing from evil and following after virtue." For example, a man formerly was very proud; now he is humble. He often used to hate others; now he loves others. He was habitually quick-tempered and easily angered; now his temperament has become slow, and he is no longer quick-tempered. All these can be considered the improvement of behavior. When a man's behavior is thus improved, is this the growth of life? No!

Why do we say growth of life is not the improvement of

behavior? It is because behavior and life are things which definitely belong to two different worlds.

Just as evil is other than life, so also is good other than life. Just as evil is not life, so also is good not life. Evil and good, though different in nature, are of the same world; both are other than life, and both are not life. Thus, in the Bible, good and evil are not two trees, but one tree; life is another tree, being something of another world, another kingdom (Gen. 2:9). We can say that good and evil on one hand and life on the other hand definitely belong to two different categories. Thus, a man, by his own determination and effort, can improve considerably in behavior and yet still be very immature and weak in the life of God. This is because his improvement is entirely apart from life; it is of his own work and not of life. Besides, what he has improved is not the result of his growth in life. Therefore, growth of life is not the improvement of behavior.

II. GROWTH OF LIFE
IS NOT THE EXPRESSION OF PIETY

What is the expression of piety? The expression of piety differs from improvement of behavior. Improvement of behavior is toward men, which means a person's behavior and character before men has been improved and becomes better than before. The expression of piety is toward God, which means a person's attitude before God is full of reverence and fear, besides being devout and sincere. Yet whether it be the improvement of behavior or the expression of piety, both alike are not the growth of life. Some believers may be very reverential and devout before God; they dare not be disrespectful or loose in their behavior and action. We cannot say these expressions are not good, but neither are they the growth of life. This is because such believers only look upon God as One who is high above all, One who is worthy of reverence and fear; therefore, they have a heart of veneration and the expression of piety. Yet as to how God in Christ dwells in man as man's life, and how by the working of the law of this life He is within man to be God to man, they may not have the slightest knowledge nor the slightest experience. Though they have the expression of piety, yet such expression is not due to the growth of the life of God within them; therefore, it is not an indication that they have the growth of life within them. Hence, growth of life is also not the expression of piety.

III. GROWTH OF LIFE
IS NOT ZEALOUS SERVING

What is zealous serving? This means that formerly a believer was indifferent and cold toward the things of God; now he is enthusiastically pressing on in serving God. Or formerly he seldom came to the meetings, and now he is present at every meeting. Formerly he was not concerned about the church; now he participates in all kinds of services of the church. Though such zealous serving manifests a believer's fervency toward the Lord and his diligence in serving the Lord, and though it is also often commended by men, yet such zeal may very possibly be mixed with much human excitement, busyness, and interest. It is also quite possible that such serving is according to the soulish power of man and depends on the strength of man; it is not from the leading of the Holy Spirit; even less does it depend on the life of Christ or help men to have a deeper union with God. Hence, such zealous serving does not come from life and is not of life; therefore, it is not the growth of life.

We see in the Bible that before the apostle Paul was saved, he served God with zeal (Acts 22:3). At that time, though within him he had not received the life of God, he could serve God outwardly by his own excitement and strength in a very zealous manner. This shows us that zealously serving God may be wholly unrelated to life. It does not indicate one iota the condition of a person's life. Therefore, growth of life is also not zealous serving.

IV. GROWTH OF LIFE
IS NOT THE INCREASE OF KNOWLEDGE

Though the increase of a believer's spiritual knowledge through hearing more messages, knowing more truths, understanding more of the Bible, and comprehending more spiritual terms, etc., is a kind of growth, yet it is not growth of life. The increase of such knowledge only causes his mind to become improved and more thoroughly versed, and his head to have more comprehension or more ability to comprehend. It is not that the Holy Spirit has given greater revelation within him or that life has gained more ground within him so that he has growth in the real knowledge and experience of Christ as life. The increase of such knowledge alone simply causes men to be puffed up (1 Cor. 8:1). It is nothing before God (1 Cor. 13:2) and has no value in life. Thus, growth of life is not the increase of knowledge.

V. GROWTH OF LIFE
IS NOT TO ABOUND IN GIFTS

Though it is quite precious for a believer to abound in spiritual gifts, such as the ability to minister, heal, speak in tongues, etc., yet this is also not the growth of life. It is the miraculous power of the Holy Spirit descending more upon a believer which causes him to have such gifts. It is not because the life of God has grown and matured within him that the gifts are manifested. It is possible, on the one hand, that a man who is used by the Holy Spirit may manifest more gifts; yet, on the other hand, he may not have allowed the Holy Spirit to have more of the life of God wrought into him. Thus, abounding in gifts does not necessarily mean growing in life.

The believers in Corinth were enriched in all utterance and all knowledge and came behind in no gift (1 Cor. 1:5, 7), yet in life they were still very immature; indeed they were carnal and babes in Christ (1 Cor. 3:1). This shows us that growth of life is also not to be abounding in gifts.

VI. GROWTH OF LIFE
IS NOT THE INCREASE OF POWER

It is possible that a believer may be more powerful than before in serving God; in preaching or in testifying, he is able to move men more than before; in administering the church or in managing the affairs, he has more wisdom than before. These are an increase in power, but they are still not growth in life. Such increase of power is but an outward power which the Holy Spirit has bestowed on him. It is not that the Holy

Spirit has interwoven life within him, and thus, through his spirit, manifested life power from within him; therefore, it is neither from life nor of life. Thus, the increase of such power is also not the growth of life.

Luke 9 tells us that in the beginning, all the twelve disciples who followed the Lord received power and authority from the Lord so that they could subdue all kinds of demons and heal all kinds of diseases; yet at that time the condition of their spiritual life was very immature. This suffices to show us that the increase of power is not the growth of life.

From these six negative points, we see that it is not by being improved in our behavior, by having an expression of piety before God, by being zealous in serving God, by increasing our spiritual knowledge, by abounding in outward gifts, or by our power in work being augmented that we have growth in life. None of these are the growth of life. It is a pity that almost all Christians today take these as standards for the growth of life. They determine whether or not there is growth of life in a Christian by looking at his behavior, piety, zeal, knowledge, gifts, and power. Such a way of evaluating things is not accurate. Copper is very much like gold, yet it is not gold. Likewise, though these six points somewhat resemble the growth of life, they are not growth of life. Of course, real growth of life will manifest these six points to some extent; yet to measure growth of life merely by these six points is not right.

Then, after all, what is the growth of life? This requires that we consider the matter again, this time from the positive side:

I. GROWTH OF LIFE IS
THE INCREASE OF THE ELEMENT OF GOD

The increase of the element of God means that more of God Himself is blended into us, is gained by us, and has become our element. We have said that life is God Himself, and to experience life is to experience God; therefore, the growth of life is the increase of the element of God in us, until all that is of the Godhead is completely formed in us that we may be filled unto all the fullness of God (Eph. 3:19).

II. GROWTH OF LIFE IS
THE INCREASE OF THE STATURE OF CHRIST

While life is God Himself, God being our life is Christ; therefore, the Bible says that Christ is our life. We can say that when we are regenerated, it is Christ being born again within us to be our life. But when we first receive it, this life is still very young and immature, which means that the stature of Christ within us is very small. When we love Christ, seek Christ, and allow Christ to live in us more and thereby gain us, the stature of Christ gradually increases within us. This is the growth of life. Since this life is Christ who lives in us, the growth of this life is therefore the increase of the stature of Christ within us.

III. GROWTH OF LIFE IS
THE EXPANDING
OF THE GROUND OF THE HOLY SPIRIT

We have also mentioned that life not only is God, but it is Christ, and it is also the Holy Spirit. We may say that to experience life is to experience the Holy Spirit; therefore, to grow in life also means to allow the Holy Spirit to gain more ground within us. When we pursue more urgently the working of the Holy Spirit within us and give diligence in obeying the teaching of the Holy Spirit within us as the anointing, the Holy Spirit can then expand His ground extensively; thus, life within us will grow to a great extent. Therefore, the growth of life means also that the ground of the Holy Spirit has expanded within us.

IV. GROWTH OF LIFE IS
THE DECREASE OF THE HUMAN ELEMENT

The above three points reveal that if in a believer the element of God is increased, the stature of Christ is increased, and the ground of the Holy Spirit is expanded, his life then has grown. All these points speak from God's side. Now we shall speak from our side. Firstly, the growth of life is the decrease of the human element. The decrease of the human element is the decrease of Adam, the old creation, in man, which also means the decrease of the savor of man and the increase of the savor of God. Some brothers are very enthusiastic, while some sisters are very gentle; in outward appearance they seem to have grown in life, yet they are full of human element, human savor; they cannot cause you to touch the element of God or sense the savor of God. Therefore, if we wish to see whether a brother or sister has grown in life, we cannot simply observe how they behave outwardly, how devout and zealous they are, or how much knowledge, gift or power they have. Rather, we must discern whether there is the increase of the element of God within these things, or, on the other hand, still an abundance of human element. The decrease of the human element is the increase of the divine element. If a believer has really grown in life, his speech, actions, living or working must all impart the sense that they are not according to himself, but according to God; not of his own intelligence, but by the grace of God; therefore, they do not carry the savor of man, but more the savor of God, which also means that the human element has decreased and the element of God has increased. Thus, the growth of life is not only the increase of the element of God, but also the decrease of the element of man.

This point is rather important; yet it is rather difficult for brothers and sisters to apprehend. Though for more than ten years we who serve the Lord in the ministry of the word have been speaking continually in this way, we are still not able to speak this point into the brothers and sisters. We have spoken at times until all nodded their heads in agreement; yet when it came to actual practice the brothers and sisters still considered whether there was any improvement in behavior or zeal in serving, etc., as standards to determine whether there was growth in life. Once in a certain place the responsible brothers of the church spoke to me with one voice, saying, "There is a sister here who speaks and walks firmly and lightly, and who is so quiet and gentle, truly spiritual, and full of life." I then said to them, "If this is called being spiritual or having life, then the statue of Mary in the Catholic Church is even more spiritual and full of life, because it is more gentle and quiet than she." Her quietness and gentleness were full of human savor and human element; they were entirely the product of human effort. When we want to determine a believer's condition in life, we cannot go by what he manifests outwardly; we must sense the savor and the element in what he manifests. Is it the savor of God or the savor of man? Is it the element of God or the element of man? Many times our perception may not be accurate, but the smell is accurate. It is possible that a certain piece of clothing appears very clean to you, but if you take it and smell it, you will know that it is full of a filthy odor. Thus, if we want to evaluate the condition of life within a man, it should be like sampling tea: just by a little tasting, you can tell its flavor.

V. GROWTH OF LIFE IS
THE BREAKING OF THE NATURAL LIFE

The breaking of a believer's natural life is also a proof of his growth in life. The breaking of the natural life means that our own power, ability, view, and method are all so dealt with by the Holy Spirit and the cross that they are broken. For example, consider a brother who formerly in his behavior and action, in his working for the Lord, and in his administering of the church, depended on his own natural power, ability, view, and method. In all things, he relied on his own power and ability; he used his own concept and method. Later, he was dealt with by the cross and disciplined by the Holy Spirit through environment so that his natural life was somewhat broken. Now, when he comes to work and manage affairs, he does not trust in his own power, ability, view, and method. Such a man whose natural life has been broken learns no longer to rely on the power of his natural life or to live by his natural life, but he continually depends on the power of the life of God and lives by the life of God. In this way the life within him can grow. Thus, the growth of life is the breaking of the natural life.

VI. GROWTH OF LIFE IS
THE SUBDUING OF EVERY PART OF THE SOUL

When we speak of what deliverance from sin is, we should pay attention to the flesh being crucified; when we speak of what the growth of life is, we should pay attention to the soul being subdued. Positively speaking, the growth of life is the expanding of the ground of the Holy Spirit; negatively speaking, it means that every part of the soul is being subdued. Every one who lives in the natural life lives by the soul. We all know that the soul has three parts: mind, emotion, and will. Therefore, to live by the soul is to live by the mind, by the emotion, or by the will. The part of a man's soul which is particularly strong and outstanding is the very part by which that man lives; when he encounters things, he definitely uses that part to deal with them. Once Brother Nee said that it is similar to a man who carelessly walks into a wall; when he does so, his nose always hits first. Whatever part of the body stands out, that part will hit the wall first. The situation of our soul is like this. If a person's mind is particularly strong, whenever he has an encounter, his mind will definitely come first. If his emotion is particularly thriving, whenever he has an encounter, his emotion will move first. If his will is particularly strong, whenever he has an encounter, it will certainly be his will that takes the lead.

When a man has received sufficient dealings of the cross, every part of his soul is subdued. His mind, emotion, and will are all broken and subdued; they do not stand out as before. Whenever he encounters something, he is afraid to use the mind, he is afraid to use the emotion, he is afraid to use the will. The mind does not come first; the spirit comes first. The emotion does not move first; the spirit moves first. The will does not take the lead; the spirit takes the lead. This means that we should not allow the soul to take the lead, but let the spirit be in the position of the head; that we should not live by the soul, but by the spirit. Such people then have growth in life. Thus, to grow in life is to have every part of the soul subdued.

After seeing these twelve points concerning what the growth of life is, we know that the real growth of life, on our side, is a matter of decreasing, breaking, and subduing; on God's side, it is a matter of increasing, growing, and expanding. All this, we may say, is the fundamental knowledge we should have in the pursuit of life. It is also very much related to spiritual experience, which we have considered in another volume.* Therefore, we must thoroughly comprehend and accurately know all these points.

* *The Experience of Life,* published by the Living Stream Ministry.

Chapter Thirteen

THE OUTLET OF LIFE

Now we shall see the thirteenth main point concerning the knowledge of life: the outlet of life. If we want to know the way of life and pursue after the growth of life, we must be clear about the outlet of life, the way through which life comes out from within us.

Almost every main point in this chapter has already been mentioned in the previous chapters. Now we shall again consider each point specifically.

I. THE PLACE WHERE LIFE IS—THE SPIRIT

God regenerates us through His Spirit, and, by this, His life is brought into our spirit; therefore, our spirit is the place where life is.

When the life of God, which is in the Spirit of God, enters into our spirit, these three are mingled as one and become what Romans 8:2 calls "the Spirit of life." Hence, this three-in-one spirit of life within us is the place where life is.

II. THE EXIT OF LIFE—THE HEART

In the chapter *The Law of Life,* we have said that the heart is the entrance and exit of life as well as the switch of life; therefore, the heart is very closely related to the growing out of life.

Matthew 13 is the place in the Bible which says distinctly that the heart is related to the growing out of life. The Lord tells us there that life is the seed and the heart is the ground; therefore, the heart is the place where life grows out from within us. Whether or not life can grow out from within us depends entirely on the condition of our heart. If the heart is proper or upright, life can grow out; but if the heart is improper or crooked, life cannot grow out. Thus, if we want life to grow out from within us, we must deal with our heart.

Matthew 5:8 says, "Blessed are the pure in heart; for they shall see God." This tells us that our heart needs to be pure. To deal with our heart is to deal with the purity of our heart, that is, to cause our heart to desire God, love God, and incline toward God in simplicity, having no other love or desire beside God. When our heart is dealt with and becomes pure, then it is proper and upright. In this way life can grow out.

III. THE PASSAGE OF LIFE

Though the heart is the outlet of life, the place where life grows out, yet if life is to grow out from the heart, it must pass through the conscience, emotion, mind, and will—the four parts of the heart. Therefore, these four parts become the places through which life passes. Thus, we must see the relationship between each of these four parts and the growing out of life.

A. Conscience

When life grows out from within us, it passes through our conscience. The conscience needs to be without offense. To deal with the conscience is to make the conscience without offense.

Before we were saved, while we were yet sinners, we often offended God and wronged men in our conduct and behavior; our heart was filthy and deceitful; therefore, the conscience, being darkened, was full of offenses and leakages and was extremely unclean. Hence, as soon as we are saved, we should deal with the conscience. When we were first saved, a major portion of the lessons we learned, such as making restitution for past debts, clearing our old living, etc., was to cause us, even from the outset of following the Lord, to deal adequately with the conscience that it be clean and without offense. Afterwards, during our entire life of following the Lord, we might fail at times and become weak, thereby falling into sin and the flesh or becoming contaminated and occupied by the world, thus again causing our conscience to have both

offenses and leakages; therefore we need to deal continually
with our conscience that it may be kept constantly free of
offense. First Timothy 1:19 says: "Holding…a good conscience;
which some having thrust from them made shipwreck concerning the faith." This shows us that dealing with the
conscience is very much related to the growth of life. Whenever
we thrust aside the conscience and neglect the conscience, life
is immediately blocked and imprisoned. Therefore, if we
desire to have growth in life, if we want the life within us to
have an outlet and grow out from our heart, it is imperative
that we deal with the conscience.

To deal with the conscience means to deal with all
the offenses and the restless and uneasy feelings of the conscience. Before God, whether we become unrighteous because
of sin, unholy because a part of the world has occupied our
heart, or uneasy because of other inharmonious conditions,
our conscience condemns us within, thus causing us to have
feelings of offense and uneasiness before God. If we want
to deal with the conscience, we must pay attention to such
consciousnesses in the conscience. Therefore, to deal with
the conscience is to deal with these consciousnesses in the
conscience. When we have dealt thoroughly with them, our
conscience can be exceedingly clean and secure, having neither offense nor accusation. In this way life can naturally
grow out from within us.

In our actual experience, in order to deal with the conscience so that it is wholly clean, there is often a situation of
overdoing the matter. This means that the conscience is being
dealt with so that it becomes overly sensitive, almost to the
extent of being weak. In this condition, one dares not move or
act; with each move comes the feeling of offense, and with
each act comes the sense of restlessness. This seems to be a
case of going too far; yet it is necessary in the initial stage of
learning to deal with the conscience.

The period which I dealt with my conscience most severely
was in 1935. At that time, I appeared to be a mental case. For
example, when I went to others' homes, after entering the
gate, if no one came to open the door, I dared not open it and
enter in. Once I entered into the living room, if no one invited

me to sit down, I dared not sit down; and if I did, within me I would feel that I was infringing on another's sovereignty. If there were newspapers before me, if no one invited me to read them, I also dared not read them, and if I did, I would also feel within me that I was infringing on another's sovereignty. At that time, when I wrote a letter, I had to write it three or four times. The first time I wrote, I felt some words in it were not accurate, so I tore it up and wrote again. After the second writing, I again felt some words were not fitting, so I tore it up and wrote the third time. I also dared not speak to others. If I spoke, I felt there were some mistakes: either what I said was not accurate, or I spoke too much; and if I did not deal with it, I could not be at ease.

Once in Shanghai I lived with another brother in a small room. When we washed our face, we had to bring water to our room and wash. That room was very narrow; even if we were very careful, we could not help splashing a few drops of water on the other person's bed. At that time, I often splashed water on that brother's bed. Though after a little while the water dried, and strictly speaking it could not be counted as a sin, yet my conscience simply was not at ease and had a feeling of offense. I could only confess to him and apologize, saying: "Brother, please forgive me, I just splashed quite a few drops of water on your bed." When I confessed in this way, my conscience was again not at ease. It clearly was only three drops of water; how could I say "quite a few drops"? I could only confess again. In the afternoon, I was a little careless: I stepped on his shoes underneath his bed, and again my conscience would not let me go. I had to confess again. Daily from morning till night, I was dealing with this kind of sins. Eventually that brother became very impatient, and I was also embarrassed to make further confessions; yet if I did not confess, it would not do. One day, there was another offense; if I confessed to him, I feared he might lose patience; if I did not confess, I could not be at ease. At night, after the meal, he wanted to take a walk, and I offered to go out with him. I then found a chance to tell him, saying: "I was wrong again, please forgive me." Then the brother said: "The worst person is one who does wrong, but would not confess. The best person is one

who does not do wrong and does not confess. One who is neither good nor bad is one who does wrong and also confesses."
After I heard that, I said in my heart: "Lord, have pity on me!
I would not want to be the worst person, and I cannot be the
best person; I can only be a person who is neither bad nor
good."

During that time, I really dealt too much with my conscience. Yet now as I look back, that was still necessary.
Indeed, one who wants to have real growth in life must pass
through a period of dealing with the conscience in such a
severe way. If the conscience is not dealt with adequately, life
cannot grow properly.

When our conscience has passed through such severe and
thorough dealings, its consciousness is more and more sensitive. It is like the glass of a window: when it is covered with
dust and dirt, light cannot penetrate; but if we rub it a bit, it
is a little clearer. The more we rub it, the clearer it becomes,
and the more it allows the light to come through. Dealing
with the conscience is like this. The more the conscience is
dealt with, the clearer and brighter it becomes and the more
sensitive its consciousness is.

The more sensitive the conscience is, the softer is the
heart, because in every softened heart the conscience is most
sensitive. If only there is a little consciousness, it can sense it
immediately. We may say that a sensitive conscience definitely belongs to a softened heart. All whose heart is
hardened have a numb conscience. The more numb a person's
conscience is, the more hardened his heart is. Therefore,
when the Holy Spirit wants to soften our heart, He always
moves our conscience first. When preaching the Gospel we
always speak of sin; this is because our intention is to move
man's conscience so that man may feel he has many wrongs
and offenses. When man's conscience is moved, his heart is
also softened; then he is willing to receive the Lord's salvation.

Since a sensitive conscience which is without offense can
soften the heart, it naturally can allow life to grow out from
us. Thus, the conscience is the first place through which life

passes when it grows out, or the first section of the outlet for the growing out of life.

B. Emotion

When life grows out from within us, the second place through which it passes is the emotion of our heart. With the emotion of the heart, it is a question of love. To deal with the emotion is to cause our emotion to fervently love the Lord.

We know that whatever a man does, the most important question is whether he likes it or not. If he likes it, he is willing and happy to do it; if he does not like it, he is neither willing nor happy to do it. If we would allow the life of the Lord within us to grow out freely, it also requires that we be happy to cooperate with Him and willing to let Him work. Therefore, when God wants to work on us, He often moves our emotion first to make us willing to cooperate with Him. Many places in the Bible speak of loving the Lord. They are all mentioned with the intention of moving our emotion. For example, in John 21, the Lord said to Peter: "Lovest thou me more than these?" This means that the Lord wanted to move the emotion of Peter; He desired that Peter would love Him so completely that His life could have a way out from him. Again, in Romans 12:1-2, the apostle Paul says: "I beseech you...by the mercies of God, to present your bodies a living sacrifice...that ye may prove what is the...will of God." When he speaks here of the mercy of God, it is also to move our emotion, to make us love the Lord, want the Lord, seek after the Lord, and consecrate ourselves to the Lord; then we can understand the things of God. These examples show us that if we want the life of the Lord to have an outlet from within us, besides a conscience without offense, we also need an emotion which fervently loves the Lord.

The emotion which really loves the Lord is intimately related to our heart and our conscience. First Timothy 1:5 says, "The end of the charge is love out of a pure heart and a good conscience..." This passage speaks of emotion, heart, and conscience together. Paul's intention here was to tell Timothy that much of the talking of men does not count, but that love and love alone is the end of all. Yet where does this love

come from? It comes out of a pure heart and a good conscience. Thus, it is necessary to have a pure heart and a good
conscience before love can be produced. For this reason, when
we help others, we must first help them to deal with their
heart and their conscience. When the heart and the conscience are dealt with, the emotion can easily love the Lord
and want the Lord. When there is love in the emotion, it
affords an outlet to the life of God from our spirit. Thus, emotion is the second place through which the growing out of life
passes, or the second section of the outlet for the growing out
of life.

C. Mind

The third part through which the growing out of life
passes is our mind. The mind needs to be renewed. To deal
with the mind means to have our mind renewed and delivered
from all the old thoughts. Romans 12:2 says, "Be not fash-
ioned according to this age: but be ye transformed by the
renewing of your mind, that ye may prove what is the good,
and acceptable, and perfect will of God." This indicates that
only when we have a renewed and transformed mind can we
understand the will of God and allow the life of the Lord to
pass through and grow out naturally. Thus, the mind is also
intimately related to the growing out of life.

All the renewing work in our entire person is done by
the Holy Spirit (Titus 3:5). Therefore, when speaking of the
renewing of the mind, we still must begin with the work of
the Holy Spirit. We know that the beginning of the work
of the Holy Spirit within us is to regenerate us. After this,
much of the continuing working of the Holy Spirit within us
is to renew us. The Holy Spirit regenerating us causes us to
receive the life of God and have the nature of God. The Holy
Spirit renewing us causes us to know God, or to understand
the will of God and have the mind of God.

The parts within us which the Holy Spirit in His renewing
work renews are the spirit and the mind. In the chapter
entitled *The Inward Knowledge* we have made it clear that if
we want to know God, it is accomplished on our part by the
spirit and by the mind. First we obtain the knowing of the

intuition in the spirit, and then we gain the comprehension in the mind; by this we understand the will of God and know God. Thus, the spirit and the mind can be said to be one set of organs for us to know God. To have the spirit alone is not sufficient; to have the mind alone is also not enough. We must have both the spirit and the mind. It is like a light bulb shining forth with electric light. The light bulb alone is not sufficient; the filament alone is also not enough. It requires both to work together. Since the Holy Spirit's renewing is for the purpose of our knowing God, He must naturally renew the set of organs for knowing God, namely, our spirit and our mind.

Ephesians 4:22-23 says, "That ye put away, as concerning your former manner of life, the old man...and that ye be renewed in the spirit of your mind." This passage, when speaking of the matter of renewing, combines the mind and spirit together and calls the spirit "the spirit of the mind." Though in the understanding of God's will, it is a matter of the mind, yet the mind itself cannot directly touch God and know God. In order to understand the will of God, we must first use the spirit to touch God and sense God; then we must use the mind to comprehend the meaning in the intuition of the spirit. Thus, in the matter of understanding the will of God, as far as the mind is concerned, it needs the cooperation of the spirit; as far as the spirit is concerned, it is joined to the mind and is of the mind. It is like the filament in the light bulb which is connected to the light bulb and also belongs to the light bulb. Hence, in this passage the Bible calls our spirit "the spirit of the mind." When the Holy Spirit renews the "spirit of our mind," it means that He renews our spirit and our mind. The Holy Spirit renews our spirit because in the matter of knowing God the spirit is of the mind; therefore, the real renewing of the mind always begins with the renewing of the spirit. The Holy Spirit first renews our spirit, and then He renews our mind; thus, the spirit of our mind is renewed.

When the spirit of our mind is thus renewed by the Holy Spirit, our spirit becomes lively and keen. Every time the Holy Spirit works and anoints, this spirit can sense and know. In the meantime, our mind is also clear and proficient; it can immediately interpret the meaning of the intuition in the spirit. In this way, we can understand the will of God. Then whatever our mind thinks and considers is on the side of the spirit; it no longer yields to the flesh to be employed by the flesh. Our mind then will no longer be a mind set on the flesh, but a mind set on the spirit. Romans 8:6 calls such a mind the "mind of the spirit." Since this mind of the spirit is constantly set on the spirit and is mindful of the spirit, it allows the life of God to grow out continuously from our spirit.

In summary, concerning the renewing of the mind, there are these three points: Firstly, Romans 12 says that the mind needs to be renewed and put off all the old thoughts; secondly, Ephesians 4 says that the mind needs the spirit to cooperate with it, to be joined as one with it so that the spirit may become "the spirit of the mind"; thirdly, Romans 8 says that the mind should stand on the side of the spirit, yield to the spirit, be of the spirit, be constantly set on the spirit, mind the spirit, and heed the move and consciousness of the spirit, thereby becoming a "mind of the spirit." When the mind is thus renewed, has the cooperation of spirit, and stands on the side of the spirit, it can allow life to pass through and grow out smoothly without hindrance. Thus, the mind is the third place through which the growing out of life passes, or the third section of the outlet for the growing out of life.

D. Will

Fourthly, the growing out of life passes through our will. We have seen that the heart needs to be pure, the conscience needs to be without offense, the emotion needs to be loving, and the mind needs to be renewed. Then, what does the will need? From the Bible, we see that the will needs to be pliable. As far as the will is concerned, it is a matter of being pliable. To deal with the will is to make our will pliable.

The will is the organ of our proposals and decisions. Whether we want or not, decide or not, all are functions of the will. When we say "I want," or "I decide," it means that our will wants, our will decides. Thus, the will is the most essential part of our whole being; it determines our actions and our moves. We may say that it is the helm of our whole person. Just as a boat turns according to the helm, so a man moves forward or backward according to his will.

The will of a man is entirely independent, entirely free. It cannot be forced or compelled to do whatever it opposes or disapproves. Just as it acts in this way toward man, so also does it act toward God. Thus, whether the life of God can grow out from within us is very much related to whether our will is pliable and surrendered. If our will is hard, obstinate, rebellious, and in all things acting according to our own ideas, there is no way for the life of God to grow out. If our will is softened, pliable, and willing to act according to the working of life, the life of God can grow out. Hence, our will is the fourth place through which the growing out of life passes, or the fourth section of the outlet for the growing out of life.

We must note that whenever we mention the heart, we refer to these various parts, either to the conscience of the heart, the emotion of the heart, the mind of the heart, or the will of the heart. When we say that a person's heart is not pure, we refer to the heart as a whole. When we say that this person's heart is without offense, without condemnation, we refer to the conscience. When we say that a person's heart loves the Lord, we refer to the emotion. When we say that a person's heart does not understand, we refer to the mind. When we say that this person's heart is hard and stubborn, we refer to the will. When we speak of dealing with our heart, we mean dealing with these five aspects of the heart.

If we can deal with our heart until it is pure, without offense, loving the Lord, clear and proficient, and pliable, then we have a heart which is useful to the life of God, and we can allow the life of God to have a clear outlet from within us.

A FINAL WORD

Having seen where life is, the exit of life, and the passage of life, we know that if we want the life of God to have a way to grow out from us, we must deal with our spirit, heart, conscience, emotion, mind, and will until there are no problems in them. This is because the life of God takes our spirit as its abode, and it takes our heart, conscience, emotion, mind, and will as the outlet. If any one of these six organs has trouble, the life of God is blocked and cannot emerge. Therefore, if we desire to seek growth in life, it really is not so simple. Not only should we touch the spirit and know the spirit; we also should deal with every part of the heart. If we fall short in any way, we will not succeed. For this reason, the brothers and sisters today who have growth in life are exceedingly few, and their growth is very slow!

Sometimes you see a brother who you cannot say does not love the Lord; in fact, he is quite good in every way. But because his mind is peculiar, his whole spiritual future is paralyzed. Some sisters have dealt with their conscience, and there is no problem with their mind; yet because they fall short in their emotion, having other loves beside the Lord, they also do not have much spiritual growth. There are some brothers who have a stubborn will in all things; they insist on their already made-up mind; they are unwilling to be corrected, and they are unable to submit to the shining of light; therefore, life also cannot get out. Thus, to deal adequately with all these parts in our actual living is really not easy. If there is one brother or sister who has no problem at all in these matters, it is really a miracle. May God have mercy on us!

Chapter Fourteen

LIGHT AND LIFE

Now we shall see the last main point concerning the knowledge of life: light and life. From both the words of God and our own experiences, we see that light is especially related to life. We may say that it is due to our being enlightened that we receive life. And the measure of life we receive corresponds exactly with the measure of our enlightenment. Only the shining of light can bring forth life, and only the shining of light can increase life. Therefore, if we want to know life, we need to see the relationship between light and life.

I. LIFE IS DIFFERENT FROM BEHAVIOR

We have said again and again that God's intention in saving us is not for us to be evil men or good men, but to be life-men or God-men. Therefore, after we are saved, we should not merely attain to the standard of morality in our behavior and live out the goodness of man, but we should reach the standard of life in our living and live out the life of God. Hence, the way we take today is not the way of self-improvement but the way of life. Our pursuits are not improvement of behavior but growth in life. In order that we may go forward in the way of life, not swerving either to the left or to the right, we must be able to distinguish the difference between life and behavior.

Life and behavior are indeed different. In the very beginning, the Bible mentions two trees in the garden of Eden: one, the tree of life, and the other, the tree of good and evil. The tree of life denotes the life of God, while the tree of good and evil denotes good and evil behavior. The tree of life and the tree of good and evil are not one tree, but two trees. This shows us that life and behavior are really two different categories of things.

We need to see what the fundamental difference between life and behavior is. Simply speaking, life is natural growth, while behavior is human work. For example, consider a house and a tree. The house is the result of conduct, the product of human work, while the tree is an expression of life, of natural growth. The doors and windows of the house are put there by work; the flowers and leaves of the tree arrive there by growth. The house which is built demonstrates a kind of behavior; the tree which has grown proves a kind of life. The difference between these two is very evident. With us as Christians, the difference between behavior and life is just like this. That which is produced by exerting our own human effort is behavior, whereas only that which is produced from the growth of the life of God within us is life. Some brothers and sisters are very loving, patient, humble and meek. At first glance, it seems that they really have life, but actually these virtues are only a certain form of behavior worked out by themselves, not life grown out from within. Though their behavior has been much improved, their life has grown but little.

Although life and behavior are indeed different, yet in outward appearance these two are often very much alike, and it is difficult to distinguish between them. How can we differentiate between life and behavior?

Firstly, we can differentiate between them by their taste or smell. A form of behavior can closely resemble life, but it definitely does not have the taste or smell of life. For example, there may be two trees which outwardly appear the same; one, however, is a real tree with life, while the other is an artificial tree without life. On the real tree with life many fruits are borne, while on the artificial tree without life someone has placed some fruits. The fruits of both trees have the same form and the same color; there is hardly any difference in outward appearance. But if we simply smell or taste the fruit, we can immediately tell the difference. The real fruit is tasteful, but the artificial fruit is tasteless; it can only afford to be

observed, not tasted. What we Christians manifest in our
daily living is also like this. With some brothers and sisters,
the form and the manner of their daily living seem very much
of life; yet if you smell carefully, there is no smell of life. Some
sisters come quite close in imitating Madame Guyon's
manner of prayer and fellowship, but the smell is not right.
Some brothers imitate the humble manners of Jesus the
Nazarene, but, though outwardly they really act the part, the
smell is missing inwardly. Such are the works of men, not the
growth of life; such is the acting out of behavior, not the living
out of life. Thus, by its taste or smell we can discern whether
a Christian's living stems from life or is merely a form of
behavior. All that stems from life has the taste or smell of life,
the taste or smell of God; if it is only behavior, it has only the
taste and smell of man.

Secondly, we can distinguish between life and behavior
through the test of environmental changes. All that stems
from life can stand the change of environment; though it suffers blows, it can still survive. It is not so with behavior. The
moment a blow comes, the behavior is either changed in
nature or is extinguished. For example, if we bury a seed of
life in the earth, it will grow and bear much fruit. But if we
bury a stone without life in the earth, nothing will issue from
it. Many times it is very difficult to distinguish whether that
which a Christian expresses is life or behavior; and at times,
it is even hard to differentiate by its taste or smell. Then we
can only let the change in environment be the test. When God
allows all kinds of enticements, temptations, difficulties, or
blows from the environment to come upon a Christian, if
what he has is from the life of God, it can still survive after
passing through all these circumstances, and it is even more
manifested. This is because the life of God contains the great
power of resurrection; it does not fear blow, destruction, or
death, and cannot be suppressed by any adverse environment; on the contrary, it breaks through all, overcomes all,
and flourishes incorruptibly forever. However, if what he has
is merely from human behavior, once it meets adverse environment, blows, destruction or trials, it changes its nature or
is extinguished. Since all human behavior issues from human

labor, it cannot stand blows or destruction; neither can it overcome temptation or tests; once the environment changes, it finds it difficult to exist in the same way.

Once there was a sister who imitated Madame Guyon to such an extent that no matter what she encountered she was never troubled; she always took everything calmly. Not only had she learned to act like Madame Guyon outwardly; even the taste or smell resembled hers. But the day came when her most beloved son, her "only son Isaac," suddenly fell ill. Then all that she had learned escaped her, and she was more anxious than anyone. This proves that when she formerly showed no anxiety, it was of human effort; therefore, it could not stand the test.

Thus, we should not hastily judge the spiritual condition of brothers and sisters, neither should we be quick to praise the expression of their living. Our observation and feeling are often not reliable. Only what God has proven by time is accurate. What is merely of human behavior will fall with the passing of time; either it will change in nature, or it will be destroyed. That which stems from the life of God, however, will survive the passing of time. This testing by time is of God; it causes us to see what is life and what is behavior.

Let me refer here to some personal matters in order to illustrate the difference between life and behavior. Soon after I believed in the Lord, I heard that those in the seminaries were pious in their daily living, behavior and attitude and were also very reverent toward the Lord. When I heard that, I admired them greatly. Later, I also heard that someone, after being saved, became an entirely different person from before. When I heard this, I was even more moved. From then on, I determined to have the pious living of the students in the seminaries. I also wanted to be a Christian who was an entirely different person from before. Thus, every day I made an effort to behave and learn. Such doing and learning did not stem from life, but was due to outward influences and the admiration in my heart. I tried my best with my own effort to imitate others; hence, it was entirely a form of behavior.

Consider another example. At that time, the custom of celebrating the new year was still very prevalent among the

Chinese. However, through the Lord's deliverance, such things had no more ground within me. In the morning of the first day of that year, after I arose, I knelt down as usual to pray and read the Bible and fully experienced the presence of the Lord. When I finished praying and had risen, my mother told me to put on the new gown which was prepared for me. I took it casually, put it on, and went with my family to eat the new year feast. When I had eaten and returned to my room, I again knelt down and prayed, but I had strangely lost the presence of God within. I felt as if God within me had left. Then I had a deep feeling that I should not have worn that gown. I immediately took it off and put on my old gown. Then again I prayed. At this time I touched the presence of God; I felt that God had returned.

Oh, brothers and sisters, this is life! This was not an outward encouragement, resolution or behavior; neither was it a teaching, practice, or imitation. It was the life of God in my deepest part giving me a certain consciousness and making known to me that I should not wear that new gown. This consciousness within was also the power of life, rescuing me. From that day forth, the custom of festivity fell completely away from me. How different this is from the previous example of outward admiration and imitation. This is the expression of life.

In 1940 in Shanghai, there was a training meeting for the co-workers, and many came. At that time a brother told me: "If the growth in life of the brothers and sisters who are staying here is not adequate, they will have to act more." These words are quite meaningful, for in that environment, one will naturally act to be a little more pious and a little more spiritual. All these activities are not life.

Whenever, because of the influence of a certain environment or due to admiration or fear, we respond with a certain way of living, such living is merely an act, a form of behavior; and one day, when the environment changes, it too will change. Thus, our living must not be the result of the influence of environment, but of the sense of life within. When the outward environment suits me, I live thus; when the outward environment does not suit me, I also live thus. The environment may change, but my living should not change. Such living then is of life.

Now that we have seen the difference between life and behavior, we should examine our own living and check it point by point. How much of it is not a performance? How much is not imitation? How much of it is lived out from the life within us? Once we examine ourselves in this way, we will immediately see that much of it is only behavior, imitation, submission and adaptation to certain outward regulations because of outward influence; very little of it is lived out by the life within. This indicates that we have not completely forsaken the behavior of human labor.

How then can we leave the behavior of human labor and live out life? We must realize that behavior is born of another's encouragement and teaching or one's own imitation or practice, whereas life springs from the enlightening of God. Behavior does not require any enlightenment; it can be worked out by human effort. Life, however, can be produced only by the shining of light. Therefore, if we want to be delivered from our behavior and live out life, we must be enlightened. Without enlightening, we can at most work out behavior; but with the shining of light, we can live out life.

II. LIFE IS FROM LIGHT

The whole Bible reveals that life comes from the shining of light. When light enters, life follows. Where light is, there life is. The amount of life is in direct proportion to the amount of light. Genesis chapters one and two say that before God began His recovery work, the entire earth was void and dark, which means that it was filled with death, for darkness is the symbol of death. Therefore, the first step of God's work was to command that there be light. When light came, it destroyed the death which belongs to darkness and began to bring in life. Thus, life follows light, and life begins from light.

The first day God commanded the light; then the plant life was brought forth on the third day. For the plant life, the light of the first day was sufficient. Yet for higher life, stronger light was required. Therefore, on the fourth day, God commanded the sun, moon and stars to shine forth. In this way, higher life was brought in. Not only were there birds, fish, beasts, and all kinds of animal life, but also the life of man, who was in the image of God. Finally, on the seventh day, God, who was represented by the tree of life, came forth. God as the highest light brought in the highest life, which is the life of God. The process of the appearing of various kinds of life shows us that life always follows light. Life begins with light, and life proceeds higher as light becomes stronger.

The light of the first day was not concrete; therefore, it brought in the plant life, the lowest life, a life which is without consciousness. This symbolizes the shining of light we received within when we were first saved (2 Cor. 4:6). Though this light brought the life of God into us, yet it only imparted to us a life in the initial stage, a life which does not have much substance and is without form.

The light of the fourth day was stronger than the light of the first day. It was more clear and definite, more concrete. Therefore, it brought in higher life, the animal life. Because the light was more substantial and strong, the life was also more substantial and high. Light progressed and, following it, life also progressed. This typifies our experience: as within us we receive stronger, clearer, more definite, and more concrete shining of light, the life within us also grows and becomes more defined in form. Thus, Christ is "formed" within us.

The light of the seventh day was the highest; therefore, it brought in the highest life, the life of God, which was represented by the tree of life. When light reached the apex, life also attained to the peak. When light becomes complete, life also becomes full. When within us the shining of light we receive has reached the apex, our spiritual life will also have become full and mature and will have reached the state of being completely like God.

In Genesis chapters one and two, the Holy Spirit continually shows us that life follows light. He shows us that light is divided into three stages—the first day, the fourth day and the seventh day; therefore, life is also divided into three stages. Light marks the beginning of each stage. The light of a particular stage brings in the life of that particular stage. The degree of light of that stage determines the degree of life it brings in.

The purpose of God was that man, who was created in the light of the fourth day, might touch the tree of life, which was manifested in the light of the seventh day, and thereby receive the uncreated life of God represented by this tree. Unfortunately, before man received this life, Satan came to tempt him. He persuaded man to receive the life of Satan, which was represented by the tree of good and evil, and thus man became corrupted. Then, since man was corrupted, God could only blockade the tree of life so that man could not touch it (Gen. 3:24). In this way, the life brought in by the light of the seventh day was put aside. Then, one day, God Himself was made flesh and came to earth to be light and life. John spoke of Him, saying, "In him was life; and the life was the light of men" (John 1:4). He Himself also said: "I am the light of the world: he that followeth me…shall have the light of life" (John 8:12). Thus, the coming of the Lord Jesus to earth meant that the light of the seventh day accompanied by the life of the seventh day was again manifested among men so that all who believe and receive Him can receive this life in them. In this way, the original intention of God is fulfilled.

In Revelation chapters twenty-one and twenty-two, the New Jerusalem appears. Within that city there is the light of the glory of God; therefore, there is no need of the light of sun and moon. There is also no longer any night. At the same time, in the midst of the street of the city, there is a river of water of life, and on both sides of the river is the tree of life. All those who are saved may freely drink of the water of life and partake of the tree of life. Thus, the interior of that city is filled with light and life. On the one hand, light chases away darkness; on the other hand, life swallows up death. This is the glorious scene when the life in the light of the seventh day is received by men and mingled with men. It is also the ultimate consummation of God being received by men as life in light.

All these passages show that there is a line in the whole Bible which continuously speaks of life and light together. Where light is, there is life. This is a great principle in the

Bible. Psalm 36:9 says, "With thee is the fountain of *life;* in thy *light* shall we see light." This also clearly speaks of the relationship between life and light. Life always follows light, and only light can bring forth life.

Therefore, if we want to know the condition of life in a man, we must see the state of the enlightenment within him. We often think that if a man becomes a little more zealous, his life has grown; or if he is a little more pious, his life is improved. Such concepts are totally incorrect. Life is not in the zeal of man; neither is it in the piety of man. There is only one realm and one source of life, and that is light. Life rests with light; life also comes from light. To determine whether a person has grown in life, we must observe the condition of his enlightenment within.

Thus, if we want to help others to grow in life, we must help them to be enlightened. If others can receive enlightenment from us, they can grow in life. For example, in the ministry of the Word, if what we say is but a kind of encouragement or teaching, it can only stir people, influence people, and cause them to improve in behavior; it cannot produce the end result of life. Our work also can only have temporary effect; its issue cannot remain long. If we ourselves have been enlightened and live in the shining of light, then the words we release can bring light, which makes manifest the actual difficulties of men. (Ephesians 5:13 refers to this when it says that all things that are reproved are made manifest by the light.) After men hear such words, they may not remember the doctrine clearly, yet deep within them there is left something living which constantly moves them, touches them, and effects changes in their daily living. Such changes are not outward reform through human effort, but are the manifestation of life from the receiving of enlightening within; therefore, the issue can endure without change.

In preaching the Gospel, the same principle applies. Some who preach the Gospel can convince men by their words; yet they cannot cause men to touch from within the shining light of the Gospel. Therefore, though a man says with his mouth that he believes and even is determined in his heart to believe, he cannot from within receive life to be born again and be saved. Nevertheless, some who preach the Gospel preach words which are full of light. While men are listening, the light of the Gospel shines into them. They may continually shake their heads and say, "I do not believe," yet after they return home, something inside continually tells them, "Believe, believe!" Then they cannot help but believe. This is the result of that shining of light which causes men to receive life from within and thus be born again and saved. These examples all reveal that life comes out of light. With light, life can be brought forth; without light, life cannot be brought forth. Life springs indeed from light.

III. LIGHT IS IN THE WORD OF GOD

Since life rests with light, with what then does light rest? From the Bible we see that light rests with the Word of God. This is also a great principle in the Bible. Psalm 119:105 says, "Thy word is a lamp unto my feet, and light unto my path." And verse 130 says, "The opening of thy words giveth light." These verses show us that light rests indeed with the Word of God. Therefore, if we want to obtain light, we must obtain the Word of God. Whenever we obtain the Word of God, we obtain light. The reason we do not have light is that we lack the Word of God.

The Word of God we speak of here does not refer to the written word in the Bible, but to the word the Holy Spirit speaks to us from within. The Bible is God's written Word; this is certainly correct. But such a Word, composed of mere fixed letters, does not have the power of shining light and cannot be light to us. However, when the Holy Spirit reveals anew the word of the Bible, opening and quickening it to us, the Word then has the power of shining light and can be our light. If we only read the Bible, though we read it thoroughly and even memorize it, what we obtain are but doctrines of letters. We have not as yet obtained the Word of God; hence we have not obtained light. Only when the Holy Spirit in our spirit gives us revelation, opening up the word of the Bible to us, does the word become the living Word of God which can cause us to obtain the light of God.

In John 6:63 the Lord says: "The words that I have spoken

unto you are spirit, and are life." Here the Lord speaks of words, spirit, and life—three things together. Since both life and spirit are within us, it is clear that the words which the Lord speaks of here must also refer to the words which are spoken within us, not the letters of the Bible without. All the words outside of us are mere knowledge, not light. Only the words which enter into our spirit are the living, shining words of God. If when we read the Bible we constantly exercise our spirit in fellowship to read and open our spirit to receive, the words of the Bible are spirit and life to us. They can enter into our spirit and become living words, bringing the light of life.

Since light is in the Word of God, we must respect the Word of God. Whenever the Holy Spirit speaks to us from within, we should absolutely obey and not be negligent or disobedient. Isaiah 66:2 says that God will look to him who trembles at His Word. And verse 5 says that he who trembles at God's Word should hear His Word. If we disobey the Word of God, we refuse the light of God. Whenever we refuse light, light disappears. When light disappears, life is also gone, the presence of the Holy Spirit and God is withdrawn, and all spiritual riches and spiritual blessings are lost as well. This is really a great loss! Thus, whenever one who really knows God touches the Word of God, he fears and trembles and dares not refuse or disobey.

If God speaks to you once and you heed not, if He speaks to you again and you disobey, if then the third time He speaks to you and you again let Him pass by, there is definitely not a bit of light within you, not the least opening, and life also has no entrance whatever. If you obey whenever God speaks to you, your experience is quite different: your first obedience to the Word of God produces an opening within through which light can shine in; and when you obey the Word of God again, there is another opening through which more light can shine in. If you continue to thus obey, you will be like the four living creatures, with the body round about full of eyes (Rev. 4:8), being so transparent, full of light and full of life. Hence, we see that life is in light, and light is in the Word of God.

IV. LIGHT IS THE INNER SENSE

We have seen that light is in the Word of God and that this Word of God refers to the word the Holy Spirit speaks to us from within; therefore, the light which we receive is not a kind of outward, objective light, but an inward, subjective light.

John 1:4 tells us that the life of God is in the Lord Jesus, and this life is the light of men. When we receive the Lord Jesus as Savior, this life enters into us and becomes our "light of life" (John 8:12). Therefore, strictly speaking, this light is not an objective light which enlightens us from without, but a subjective light which enlightens us from within.

Ephesians 1:17-18 says that as we receive the spirit of revelation, the eyes of our understanding are enlightened, which also means that we receive the shining of light within. Since revelation of the Holy Spirit is an inward, subjective matter, the light brought by this revelation must definitely not be an objective light outside of us, but a subjective light within us.

Since the light is within us, every time the light shines it causes us to have a certain consciousness within. Thus, we may say that light is our inner sense. Consider the example of my wearing the new gown at new year's time. When I wore the new gown, I felt no peace within. That feeling was the inner enlightening. Thus, the light within is the sense within, and the sense within is also the light within. More than ten years ago, we seldom used this word, *sense*. Now we are very clear that if we speak of the shining of light, we cannot avoid speaking of a sense, because all the sense we have within is the enlightening we obtain.

Today, whether we are in light or darkness, whether we have been enlightened much or little, depends on the condition of the consciousness within us. A person without consciousness is in darkness and does not allow the light of God to shine within him. A person with consciousness is in the light and allows the light of God to shine within him. Thus, a person who is full of consciousness is full of light and transparent.

There are some brothers and sisters whose condition before the Lord is like this. When others contact them, they feel that they are transparent and clear as crystal. I was told that there was a brother who, whenever he spoke, gave others the feeling that he was transparent. This word is true. When some speak, you feel that they are not transparent. Others, you feel, have a little light within, but are not quite transparent. And still others, as soon as they arise and speak, impart the sense that they are completely transparent. They are like this because they are full of inner sense. It is always such that the more consciousness a man feels, the more transparent he is.

How can we be full of this sense and become transparent? This depends on how we treat the Holy Spirit when He enlightens us and gives us consciousness. If we do not obey the consciousness given by the Holy Spirit, we will not be transparent within, and our sense will become unavoidably slow and dull. If we disobey again and again, the consciousness within will become more dull, more dim, as time goes on until it is completely darkened, having no feeling at all. If we are willing to continually obey the consciousness which the Holy Spirit gives, the Holy Spirit will gain increasing ground within us and have increasing opportunity to work; the enlightening within will become brighter and brighter, and the consciousness will be increasingly richer and more sensitive.

V. ENLIGHTENING RESTS WITH THE MERCY OF GOD

How can we receive enlightening? What does enlightening depend upon? Speaking from God's side, enlightening rests absolutely on the mercy of God. He will have mercy on whom He will have mercy, and He will have compassion on whom He will have compassion (Rom. 9:15). He who receives revelation is the one to whom God gives revelation. He who obtains enlightening is the one whom God enlightens. It is entirely up to God; it is not up to us. Hence, no one can demand light, and no one can control light. When light comes, it comes without your seeking it. When light does not come, even if you seek it, it does not come. It is just like the rising of the sun. When the sun rises, it rises. You may not want it to rise, but it will not listen to you. When the sun does not rise, it does not rise; though you may want it to rise, it will not listen to you. Likewise, if God enlightens us, we can be enlightened; but if God does not enlighten us, there is nothing we can do. One day on the road to Damascus, Saul, who had opposed God, had no heart to seek light; yet the light from heaven fell upon him, causing him to prostrate himself and be greatly blessed (Acts 9:3-4). God had mercy on him. Thus, the light of God is not controlled by the hand of man, but by the hand of God. It absolutely rests upon the mercy of God.

Therefore, if we want to be enlightened, we can only wait for God, look unto Him, and trust in Him; there is not a bit more that we can do. When we do other things, we can decide by ourselves, but we cannot decide to be enlightened. We cannot say that such and such a brother knows how to read the Bible, and I also know how to read the Bible; he can receive light from the Bible, and I also can receive light from the Bible. It is difficult for all who are thus minded to obtain light.

Some may say that though we cannot control natural light, we can make light of our own by means of electricity or by burning oil lamps or candles. However, if we wish to be enlightened in spiritual matters, we cannot do this. We can only wait for God to shine. If God does not enlighten us, we definitely should not manufacture light ourselves nor seek light ourselves. Concerning this matter, Isaiah 50:10-11 says: "Who is among you that feareth Jehovah, that obeyeth the voice of his servant? he that walketh in darkness, and hath no light, let him trust in the name of Jehovah, and rely upon his God. Behold, all ye that kindle a fire, that gird yourselves about with firebrands; walk ye in the flame of your fire, and among the brands that ye have kindled. This shall ye have of my hand; ye shall lie down in sorrow." In the entire Bible, this is the passage which speaks most clearly concerning the matter of being enlightened. On one hand, it points out to us the proper way: if we fear God, obey God's voice, and suddenly fall into darkness and have no light, we should not do anything but trust in the name of the Lord, rely upon our God, and wait for the light of God to shine. This is because only God is light, only God is the source of light, and only in the light of God can we see light. On the other hand, this verse also warns us that when we have no light we should not find a way out ourselves by kindling a fire or making our own light. For if we do not wait for God, but instead gird ourselves about with self-made light, though we may walk in the light of our own fire for a time, in the end we shall lie down in sorrow.

At the same time, we also cannot borrow the light of others, taking the light others have received as our own for our use. For example, suppose that someone in a fellowship meeting has testified how, when encountering difficulties, he accepted the dealing of the cross and was thus blessed by God. A certain brother, after hearing such testimony, may be greatly moved, and, upon returning home, may determine from that day forward to accept the dealing of the cross. Though this is neither seeking light by oneself nor manufacturing light by oneself, it is borrowing light from others; it is taking the light that others have received as one's own. He who does this, after not too long a time, will definitely abandon such light. Thus, borrowed light has no use; it cannot take the place of real light.

Those among us who fear God, hear His voice and encounter darkness, should remember not to do anything but trust in God, rely upon God, look wholeheartedly to Him, wait quietly on Him, and seek His mercy once more. Whenever God comes, whenever God bestows mercy, the light of His countenance is our light, His appearing is our vision, and His presence is our gain. If we just touch Him, we see light. The moment He hides His face from us, we are immediately in darkness. No matter how much we strive for light, it is of no use; regardless of how much we struggle, it is in vain. It is not that you are a little loose, so you cannot see light, and that I am a little pious, therefore, light comes; or that you are a little lazy, so you cannot see light, and I am a little diligent, therefore, I see light. Enlightening does not depend on our striving and struggling, but on the mercy of God. Alas, how many there are today who make their own light by lighting lamps and kindling fires. When darkness comes, they do not wait till dawn, till the sun rises; they themselves go to kindle a fire, to make light themselves. God says that all those who kindle a fire to enlighten themselves shall end in sorrow. This is God's decree. What a serious matter this is! May we submit ourselves to fear God and look to Him for mercy.

VI. THE WAY TO BE ENLIGHTENED

Since enlightenment rests wholly in the controlling hand of God and depends entirely upon His mercy, should we then be completely passive and indifferent? No, not at all. From the teaching of the Bible and our own experiences, we see that we still bear responsibility. Second Corinthians 4:6 says: "Seeing it is God, that said, Light shall shine out of darkness, who *shined* in our hearts..." This verse tells us that God has already had mercy on us, has already shined on us. The God who shines in our heart is our light. As long as we are saved, we already have God within us, and we already have light. Therefore, the question now is not how we may ask for light or seek light, but how we may obtain enlightening or how we may allow the light to shine. When the sun has already risen, we do not need to seek the sun again; we only need to receive its shining. Only fools look for the sun when it is already past daybreak. Ephesians 5:14 says, "Awake, thou that sleepest, and arise from the dead, and Christ shall shine upon thee." You only need to awake; then you will receive the shining. Thus, enlightening is a matter of obtaining, a matter of accepting; it is not a matter of demanding or seeking. The responsibility we bear is to remove the coverings in order to accept light and be one who is enlightened. This includes at least the following points:

Firstly, we must want the shining. Since light depends not on our asking or seeking, but upon our accepting and receiving, then whether we are willing to accept and receive is the first condition of our being enlightened. The sun has already risen; therefore, you need not seek or ask; you only need to be shined upon by the light and receive the shining of light. If you are not willing to receive the shining, if you do not want to be shined upon, but continually cover yourself, then even if there is sun every day, it still cannot shine on you. The light of life is also like this; it has already shined within us. Today, it is not that we wait for the light, but that the light is waiting for us. The light is within us, constantly waiting for us to receive its shining. Therefore, if we want the shining and accept the shining, we can be enlightened. If we do not want it and do not accept it, it is difficult for us to be enlightened.

Very few today really want the shining. Some do not want it because they are indifferent in heart, and others do not want it because they have made up their mind to reject it. Thousands of things have become veils to the light within us. If we are not willing to remove the veils, we are those who do not want the shining and refuse it. Naturally, then, there is no way for us to be enlightened. For example, in the morning when we read the Bible and pray, if we really want the shining, it will definitely come. When the shining comes, then we can see something inwardly. This seeing is our inner sense. Whenever we have a certain consciousness deeply within us, it is a proof that the shining of light has come. The question now is whether we obey the consciousness of this shining. If we obey the consciousness of this shining and have certain dealings, then we remove the veils from us. Thus, we are those who want the shining and accept the shining of light, and we will continually have the shining. If we do not deal according to the sense of the shining, it means that we are not willing to remove the veils from us. Then we are those who do not want the shining, who refuse the shining of light. Thus, we cannot obtain the shining.

Secondly, we should open ourselves to the Lord. The Lord is light, so if our whole heart is turned toward Him, we definitely will have light; but if we turn away from Him and incline toward other things, we definitely will not have light. Second Corinthians 3:16 says, "Whensoever it (the heart) shall turn to the Lord, the veil is taken away." When the heart is not turned toward the Lord, the veil is there; but when it shall turn to the Lord, the veil is taken away. Then one can see the Lord face to face; then one can see light. Therefore, if we want to receive the shining, we must open ourselves to the Lord and, from deep within, release ourselves, putting ourselves before the Lord without a bit of reservation or hold-ing back. Thus, it will be very easy to obtain light.

But, the problem is that it is not easy for us to open our-selves toward the Lord. We still often hide ourselves; we still hold back. Not only do we dare not open ourselves to the Lord; we even dare not to pray to the Lord. It is like a child who is sometimes afraid to see his parents' face. When his parents call him, he answers with his mouth; yet he is not willing to come, for behind their back he has done things which he cannot tell. Oh, there are many whose condition before the Lord is like this. Because they have things and affairs which are not pleasing to the Lord, they hide themselves and hold back. They fear that the Lord might touch these things and affairs—then what would they do? The Lord might want them to deal with such things and affairs—then what would they do? The Lord might want them to submit to Him some-thing which they treasure—then what would they do? Since they are so afraid of being enlightened by the Lord, they dare not open themselves to the Lord. Hence they are like a piece of paper which is tightly rolled up, never willing to unfold and allow God to write the words He wants to write.

Though such people who are not willing to open to the Lord still use their mind to listen to messages and read the Bible, the messages they hear and the Bible they read only become a reference for them to judge others, an instru-ment to criticize others, while they themselves receive not a bit of light. This situation is like a man who is in a room at night. If the room is bright, he cannot see clearly the things outside; if the room is dark, he can see the things outside very clearly. Likewise, those who close themselves to the Lord are experts in judging and criticizing others. They are very clear about others' condition, but they do not know a bit concerning their own condition. This proves that they are entirely in darkness!

Such who are not willing to open themselves to the Lord can even preach and work for the Lord. Though they them-selves are not willing to accept the shining, they can persuade others to seek the shining. Though they often hope the Lord will be gracious to them and give them abundant life, equipping them and bestowing gifts on them so they can minister and work, they are afraid of the Lord's shining and even refuse the Lord's shining. Thus, the words they minister and works they do are but dead exhortations which cannot impart to men the living shining.

When men are thus unwilling to open themselves to the Lord, they become inwardly waste and void, dark and without light. It is like being in the cellar: no matter how strong the light is outside, it cannot shine within. But for one who is open to the Lord, the condition is entirely different. He completely releases himself, and from inside to outside spreads all things before the Lord without any reservation, allowing the light of God to shine. Such a person will definitely and frequently obtain enlightenment. Whether it is in hearing a message or reading the Bible, as soon as he receives the shining of light, he humbly accepts it, on the one hand being sorrowful and on the other hand worshipping the Lord. He is sorrowful because of his own desolation and failure; he worships the Lord because of His mercy and the shining of God. Being in the light, he does not see others' faults, but only his own deficiencies. Thus, he does not condemn others; he only feels that he himself is a most pitiful person, like a worm or a maggot, which cannot lift up its head before the holy Lord. He also looks to God for mercy, asks God to save him, and is willing to receive deeper shining of light. In this way, the light of God continually enlightens him within, and the life of God continually grows within him. He then becomes a transparent person, full of consciousness.

Thirdly, we should put a stop to ourselves. What does it mean to put a stop to ourselves? It is to put a stop to our views, our ways of looking at things, our feelings, opinions and words, etc. We all know that to stop is not an easy matter. There are only a very few who can really stop in this way. Yet being unable to put a stop to ourselves is also a veil, a serious veil, which prevents us from being enlightened.

For example, some brothers when reading the Bible always read with their own feelings and ideas and put their own thoughts into its meaning. The Bible clearly says, "Simon Peter," but when they read it, it becomes "Peter Simon." The

Bible clearly says, "Paul, the apostle of Jesus Christ," but when they read it, it becomes "Paul, the apostle of Christ Jesus." When they are not reading the Word of God, their opinions are not in evidence; but as soon as they read the Word of God, their opinions arise. Therefore, whenever they read the Bible, there is not one passage concerning which they do not have an opinion and feeling; yet they know not that such opinions and feelings are all wood, hay and stubble, of no value. Some brothers are like this in their ministry. When they are preaching, their words fly all over the sky, without a central or main point. Some brothers and sisters, when listening to the ministry, simply miss all the important and essential points, even after many repetitions. Yet they remember clearly the fragments, the nonessential words, which people normally forget after speaking. This also is because they have many thoughts and feelings which they cannot stop. Such brothers and sisters who are always extremely busy outwardly and indulge in fancy imaginations inwardly cannot stop any part of their entire being. Consequently they cannot obtain one bit of light.

In the New Testament there is such an example. Luke 10 and John 11 both speak of one who was most busy and could not be stopped: Martha. Luke 10 records how busy she was outwardly, while John 11 records how active she was inwardly. We may say that her whole person was in a flurry. Not only did she have many opinions and feelings, but she also had many words; she could not be stopped for a moment. Therefore, not one word of what the Lord spoke to her could enter into her. When she met the Lord, before the Lord could open His mouth, she opened hers and blamed the Lord, saying, "Lord, if thou hadst been here, my brother had not died." The Lord replied, "Thy brother shall rise again." Then she immediately had an opinion and answered, "I know that he shall rise again in the resurrection at the last day." She expounded the Lord's words so wonderfully that the time of resurrection was put off till several thousand years later. Again, the Lord said to her, "I am the resurrection, and the life: he that believeth on me, though he die, yet shall he live; and whosoever liveth and believeth on me shall never die. Believest thou this?" She said, "Yea, Lord: I have believed that thou are the Christ, the Son of God..." Her reply in no wise answered His question. She did not hear at all what the Lord had said; she was so opinionated and talkative. When she finished these words, she immediately went away, and called her sister Mary secretly, saying, "The Teacher is here, and calleth thee." This was entirely her fabrication; it was her idea put forward for the Lord. Those who are talkative and opinionated are those who can give suggestions and express opinions. Such people cannot stop a bit; thus, they are totally veiled from the light, and there is really no way for them to be enlightened.

The difficulty of being unable to stop lies within man. Many read the Bible without light and hear the ministry without grasping the essential points, not because they are sinful and worldly, but because they are full of opinions, feelings, ideas and words. Strictly speaking, sin and the world are like a piece of worn-out clothing, which is not difficult to put off. But the opinions, feelings, and ideas in us are not easy to cast off. That is why they become today the most serious veil in us; they render us unable to obtain the shining of the Lord.

Thus, if we desire to be enlightened, we must quiet ourselves and put ourselves to a stop. Not only should our outward activities be stopped; even the opinions, feelings, ideas, views and words within us should be stopped. When a person who is completely stopped comes before the Lord, he can be exceedingly simple and single in receiving the word of the Lord. Whatever the Lord says, he hears and comprehends. When he reads the Bible, he does not read his own opinion and explanation into it; rather, he reads the meaning in the Bible into himself. In the beginning, it seems that he does not understand what he reads. But when the light comes, the great things in the Bible shine in him, causing him to have revelation. The same is true when he hears a message. His whole person from within to without waits quietly before the Lord, desiring to hear His speaking. Thus, when the words are released, he can grasp the essential point of the message and receive from within the Lord's word. Such a person, because he can stop himself, is able to receive unceasingly the living Word of God, which means the light of God, for the light

of God rests within the Word of God. Thus, the third requirement for being enlightened is to stop oneself.

Fourthly, we should not dispute with light. This is another
basic requirement for being enlightened. As soon as we have
the enlightening and sense within, we should immediately
accept, submit, and deal accordingly; we cannot have any disputation. Whenever we dispute with the light, the light is
withdrawn.

When the Holy Spirit performs this enlightening work
within man, it is a very tender and delicate matter. As soon as
He meets resistance from man, He immediately withdraws.
To cause the Holy Spirit to withdraw by resisting Him is
extremely easy, but to ask Him to return is quite difficult.
Even if we confess, repent, and thereby obtain the Lord's
forgiveness, the Holy Spirit may still not come back immediately. We read of such a situation in the Song of Songs. When
the Lord knocked on His loved one's door, she did not open the
door. Later, when she realized what she had done and went to
open the door, the Lord could not be found. When the Lord
hides Himself in this way, it is His punishment toward us.

Not only does the Holy Spirit work in this way; even those
who have the ministry of the Holy Spirit work in this way. A
servant who knows God and is used by God is always happy
to help others. Yet if you criticize him or intentionally resist
him, he will not contend with you, reason with you, or argue
concerning right or wrong. He has only one way: He simply
withdraws, having nothing more to say to you and being no
longer able to help you. Thus, he who likes to contend is foolish, and the loss he suffers is tremendous! Toward one who
has the ministry of the Holy Spirit we should really be careful! You may freely criticize those who walk on the street, but
you should not freely criticize nor purposely dispute with one
who has the ministry of the Holy Spirit. This does not mean
that your criticism is not right or your disputation not reasonable; perhaps all of your criticisms are right, and all of
your disputes are reasonable; but one thing is certain: as soon
as you criticize him and dispute with him, his ministry
toward you is finished. He may be able to help thousands of
people, but he cannot help you. It is not that he would not

help you, but he cannot help you. Even if he wants to help you, you would gain nothing. What a serious matter this is! How careful we should be!

Thus, toward both the Holy Spirit who speaks within us and the ministers who speak without, we cannot engage in criticism or dispute. The enlightening of the Holy Spirit within man cannot be disputed with, for once you dispute with Him, you will be in darkness for at least several days. This period of darkness is both a punishment and reminder to you. You think it does not matter to offend God once, for you can still ask His forgiveness. Yes, He can forgive you, but God has His government; you cannot escape the punishment He has for you. And if you offend Him many times, your end will definitely be even more tragic. The people of Israel in the wilderness continually disputed with God and offended God. When they reached Kadesh-barnea, the hand of God's government came forth: they could only return to the wilderness to wander. Though they wept and repented, there was no way to restore the situation. Thus, whether it be the enlightening we receive from the Holy Spirit or the enlightening we receive from the ministers of God's Word, we should obey and not dispute. This also is a serious principle in the pursuit of spiritual things.

When the Holy Spirit enlightens us, if we are really weak and cannot submit, the most we can say is, "O God, I should obey in this matter, but I am weak; have compassion on me." This kind of heart attitude is still of His mercy. But it is best when we are enlightened to immediately submit and not dispute in the least. In this way, we can allow God to enlighten us continuously.

Fifthly, we should continuously live in the light. When in a particular matter we receive shining and thereby come to know the will of God, it is not a matter of obeying once, and that is all. We should learn to continually keep ourselves under the enlightening we have received. This means that when you receive shining in a certain matter, you should submit not only at that particular time, but you should continually submit according to that principle.

These five points are the way to obtain enlightening. If

before the Lord we pay careful attention to these five points, we can obtain frequent enlightening and live in the light. At this stage, whatever kind of guidance we need within, God will give us that kind of guidance; whatever kind of light we need, God will show us that kind of light; and whatever growth our life needs, God will, by the shining of light, cause our life to have that growth. May the Lord be gracious to us!

About the Author

Witness Lee was born in 1905 in northern China and raised in a Christian family. At age 19 he was fully captured for Christ and immediately consecrated himself to preach the gospel for the rest of his life. Early in his service, he met Watchman Nee, a renowned preacher, teacher, and writer. Witness Lee labored together with Watchman Nee under his direction. In 1934 Watchman Nee entrusted Witness Lee with the responsibility for his publication operation, called the Shanghai Gospel Bookroom.

Prior to the Communist takeover in 1949, Witness Lee was sent by Watchman Nee and his other co-workers to Taiwan to ensure that the things delivered to them by the Lord would not be lost. Watchman Nee instructed Witness Lee to continue the former's publishing operation abroad as the Taiwan Gospel Bookroom, which has been publicly recognized as the publisher of Watchman Nee's works outside China. Witness Lee's work in Taiwan manifested the Lord's abundant blessing. From a mere 350 believers, newly fled from the mainland, the churches in Taiwan grew to 20,000 in five years.

In 1962 Witness Lee felt led of the Lord to come to the United States, and he began to minister in Los Angeles. During his 35 years of service in the U.S., he ministered in weekly meetings and weekend conferences, delivering several thousand spoken messages. Much of his speaking has since been published as over 400 titles. Many of these have been translated into over fourteen languages. He gave his last public conference in February 1997 at the age of 91.

He leaves behind a prolific presentation of the truth in the Bible. His major work, *Life-study of the Bible,* comprises over 25,000 pages of commentary on every book of the Bible from the perspective of the believers' enjoyment and experience of God's divine life in Christ through the Holy Spirit. Witness Lee was the chief editor of a new translation of the New Testament into Chinese called the Recovery Version and directed the translation of the same into English. The Recovery Version also appears in a number of other languages. He provided an extensive body of footnotes, outlines, and spiritual cross references. A radio broadcast of his messages can be heard on Christian radio stations in the United States. In 1965 Witness Lee founded Living Stream Ministry, a non-profit corporation, located in Anaheim, California, which officially presents his and Watchman Nee's ministry.

Witness Lee's ministry emphasizes the experience of Christ as life and the practical oneness of the believers as the Body of Christ. Stressing the importance of attending to both these matters, he led the churches under his care to grow in Christian life and function. He was unbending in his conviction that God's goal is not narrow sectarianism but the Body of Christ. In time, believers began to meet simply as the church in their localities in response to this conviction. In recent years a number of new churches have been raised up in Russia and in many European countries.

OTHER BOOKS PUBLISHED BY
Living Stream Ministry

Titles by Witness Lee:

Abraham—Called by God	978-0-7363-0359-0
The Experience of Life	978-0-87083-417-2
The Knowledge of Life	978-0-87083-419-6
The Tree of Life	978-0-87083-300-7
The Economy of God	978-0-87083-415-8
The Divine Economy	978-0-87083-268-0
God's New Testament Economy	978-0-87083-199-7
The World Situation and God's Move	978-0-87083-092-1
Christ vs. Religion	978-0-87083-010-5
The All-inclusive Christ	978-0-87083-020-4
Gospel Outlines	978-0-87083-039-6
Character	978-0-87083-322-9
The Secret of Experiencing Christ	978-0-87083-227-7
The Life and Way for the Practice of the Church Life	978-0-87083-785-2
The Basic Revelation in the Holy Scriptures	978-0-87083-105-8
The Crucial Revelation of Life in the Scriptures	978-0-87083-372-4
The Spirit with Our Spirit	978-0-87083-798-2
Christ as the Reality	978-0-87083-047-1
The Central Line of the Divine Revelation	978-0-87083-960-3
The Full Knowledge of the Word of God	978-0-87083-289-5
Watchman Nee—A Seer of the Divine Revelation ...	978-0-87083-625-1

Titles by Watchman Nee:

How to Study the Bible	978-0-7363-0407-8
God's Overcomers	978-0-7363-0433-7
The New Covenant	978-0-7363-0088-9
The Spiritual Man • 3 volumes	978-0-7363-0269-2
Authority and Submission	978-0-7363-0185-5
The Overcoming Life	978-1-57593-817-2
The Glorious Church	978-0-87083-745-6
The Prayer Ministry of the Church	978-0-87083-860-6
The Breaking of the Outer Man and the Release ...	978-1-57593-955-1
The Mystery of Christ	978-1-57593-954-4
The God of Abraham, Isaac, and Jacob	978-0-87083-932-0
The Song of Songs	978-0-87083-872-9
The Gospel of God • 2 volumes	978-1-57593-953-7
The Normal Christian Church Life	978-0-87083-027-3
The Character of the Lord's Worker	978-1-57593-322-1
The Normal Christian Faith	978-0-87083-748-7
Watchman Nee's Testimony	978-0-87083-051-8

Available at
Christian bookstores, or contact Living Stream Ministry
2431 W. La Palma Ave. • Anaheim, CA 92801
1-800-549-5164 • www.livingstream.com